STRANGE ROADS

*Why I Turned My Back on God and
How He Finally Brought Me Home*

JADE OSTER

Strange Roads
Why I Turned My Back on God and How He Finally Brought Me Home

Disclaimer:
Many names have been changed in this book to protect both the innocent and the guilty—if only the innocent shouldn't have to suffer for the sins of the guilty! I have also changed some circumstances or combined certain events to make it harder to identify the people involved. In addition, I have excluded distinct people and incidents from my story to honor their privacy. I have only written about where our lives intersected and how that affected me. I have only shared events that are relevant to the message of this book. The stories I have written are based solely on my memories, and I am choosing to share them to the best of my ability. Due to requests for privacy from my children and my own concerns for their privacy, I have included them in my book only peripherally, mentioning them only when necessary to the context of the story. As much as I, as a proud mother, would like to expand and showcase their characters for you, dear reader, their stories belong to them, and you'll soon see why it was vital to respect their choices.
Although I have kept graphic descriptions and colorful language out of my book, this is still a book written for adults, and I have chosen to include some situations and questionable jokes of an adult nature. This may be triggering for some people.

ISBN 979-8-9928042-0-1 (paperback)
ISBN 979-8-9928042-1-8 (hardcover)

Printed in the United States of America.

What People Are Saying

"What a beautiful life lived! Jade's story is a testament to tenacity, resilience, and self-belief. Her journey inspires anyone who feels lost or overwhelmed by life's challenges."
—Wendy Beth, Soul Guide, and Author

"Jade is immensely brave and courageous to be willing to tell her story. I love her heart. It is evident from the beginning that Jade was a very hurt little girl who always wanted what was right and good. Thank you Jade for sharing, for being vulnerable, for your strong testimony."
—Karen Munson, Author

"Jade's story is a testament to the human spirit. Her candid writing invites readers to share her struggles and celebrate her growth, leaving an indelible mark of inspiration. This book is a beacon of strength for anyone facing their own battles. Her story has inspired me and given me strength and hope to persevere through my own struggles. Thank you, Jade!"
—Patti Ogden, Mother, Psychology and Social Work Double Major

"Overall, I thought Jade's story was interesting and heartfelt. She had courage in drudging up painful memories and the perseverance to make her life and the life of her children better. The message I took away from reading Jade's story was that regardless of how many sewer traps you fall in, God will pull you out if you reach out."
—Anonymous

"As Jade found forgiveness from God and from herself, she reminds us that our experiences shape our lives. Her journey helps us to know that as we learn and grow from our own experiences, we can create opportunities to start a new and fresh life. Jade's story of starting her new journey, accepting forgiveness, and remembering to forget lets the reader know that surely, we can do it too."

—Claudean Oakley, Author, Speaker and Trainer

TM

Jade Ink

"My soul's mission statement is to achieve the greatest comprehension of this universe which I live in, which others live in, and in which we act upon each other as catalysts and co-creators."

—**Jade Oster,** *written at age 12*

"And unexpectedly, I was called to be an instrument in His hands, and Lo, the fire in which He fashioned me burned hotter than the Sun and revealed the gold underneath."

—**Jade Oster,** *written at age 64*

Dedication

I have placed everything I am on the altar before Him—my whole life, all my struggles, all my mistakes, and all that I hope to be. I have given up all my sins to know Him, and I know now that my offering is acceptable unto Him.

This book is dedicated to you, my dear reader. My hope is for you to know that mercy and forgiveness have no boundaries.

Table of Contents

What People Are Saying. iii

Letter to the Reader: A Different View. 1

Prologue: What Level of Worth Are You?. 7

Chapter 1: Blood in the Water and Thirst in the Desert 13

Chapter 2: Moving Mountains, Crossing Seas 25

Chapter 3: Out of the Frying Pan 29

Chapter 4: OD Green is the New Black. 35

Chapter 5: On a White Horse. 45

Chapter 6: Bliss to Eggshells 51

Chapter 7: The Miracle. 61

Chapter 8: Good Intentions 101 67

Chapter 9: An Interesting Idea 71

Chapter 10: Running to Somewhere 83

Chapter 11: Birthday Party. 93

Chapter 12: Heartbreak World 101

Chapter 13: Lovers and Friends 111

Chapter 14: Welcome to the Jungle. 121

Chapter 15: Paging Dr. Oster. 129

Chapter 16: All the Love in the World. 137

Chapter 17: Riding the Rollercoaster 143

Chapter 18: Grace, Gratitude & Diamonds. 151

Chapter 19: Safety in the Storm 157

Chapter 20: The Road Home. 165

Chapter 21: Soul Reflections... and an Invitation 173

Epilogue: Puzzles 181

Acknowledgments 185

A Very Special Thanks 187

About the Author. 191

Reviews 195

LETTER TO THE READER:

A Different View

"You don't have a right to the cards you believe you should have been dealt. You have an obligation to play the hell out of the ones you're holding."
—**Cheryl Strayed,** Author of Wild:
From Lost to Found on the Pacific Crest Trail

Alan was sitting in his second office at home, the bathroom, as he talked to the hospital on the phone. In effect, he was doing what he does best—multitasking. I stood in the open doorway and waited for him to finish talking to the emergency room with his professional demeanor, efficiently handling crises as he did all day at work with them and all night with me at home. Everyone loves Alan's problem-solving skills.

He finished the call, placed his cell phone on the counter next to him, and returned to the task at hand.

"Alan, I need to talk to you about something," I said hesitantly.

"Sure, what's up?" he said, glancing up at me.

"I've decided to write a book. It's a memoir about my life—about growing up, my early life outside of a church, and how different my life is now that I'm a Christian. I'm also going to write about why I left the church after I first joined, what happened afterward, and why I decided to return to the church thirty years later."

"Sounds good," he said, carefully watching my face. "Soo... what's the problem?"

I swallowed. "Alan, you know my past. I've lived a big... colorful life. I've made a lot of mistakes. I've sinned a lot. While I'm not living a sinful life anymore—at least, not for the last twenty-plus years—if I write about my past, it may cause problems in how people treat us."

"I don't care," my husband said, shrugging. "Who would care? It was a long time ago."

"What if it causes problems for you at work?" I asked, my voice full of trepidation. "You're a well-respected doctor, Alan."

"I don't give a crap what anyone else thinks," he said flatly.

My husband is not a member of the church. His answer was a typical one for my Jewish comedian, physician husband. He was fiercely independent, solely focused on his work and his family.

"So, it's okay for me to tell my whole story?" I asked.

"Yeah, spit it all out, Jade. The good, the bad, and the ugly."

"There's a lot of ugly, Alan."

"I know. Just do it. Just tell what happened," he said firmly. "In fact, that's the only way to do it. Rip the Band-Aid off. Tell your story. It doesn't matter what other people think. If they don't like your book, they don't have to read it." Alan happened to think my past was one of the most entertaining and outrageous stories he'd ever heard. We'd been together for twenty-one years and married for nineteen of them.

"Did I ever tell you you're the best husband in the world?" I said, throwing my arms around him.

"Yes, you have told me," He smirked, caressing an imaginary goatee, "but not often enough."

••●••

I wish I could present a "pretty" story of my life to you, but it would not be the truth. Lies don't help anyone, and I hope to be of assistance to my reader, maybe you. I am not perfect. I have never claimed to be perfect. Except for the One exception, all humans are flawed. We each start our journey here on this rock with varying attributes, positive and negative, influenced by our DNA and natural tendencies. Then, it all gets mixed up with the cards we've each been dealt in this life. Our families of origin and our childhood experiences, our differing innate talents, along with our varying abilities and disabilities. Nature versus nurture is a delicate, sometimes explosive balance. But you still have to play the cards you've been dealt. They are the only cards you can start the game with. The hard part is that it's not under your control which cards you get.

American novelist Anne Lamott said, "You own everything that happened to you. Tell your stories." She goes on to say, "If people wanted you to write warmly about them, they should have behaved better." It's important that people be held accountable for their actions, and it's important for us to be accountable for our own.

Some of us are better at playing our hand of cards than others. I was not a skilled player when I first started, but I'm better now. I've learned the rules of the game, so I have more peace in my life. But I learned most of the rules the hard way.

As I look back on my life, I realize I have lived most of my life from a victim mentality, even a self-destructive mindset. One of my greatest learning experiences has been to grow and stretch far beyond that.

And yet, as I look back on my childhood, I can't fault the abused and victimized child for her mindset. A child has no control over the circumstances of their life. A child can't declare, "I won't put up with this!" and leave. Unfortunately, being a victim can endure well into adulthood, as abusive patterns may be recreated in various adult relationships. These patterns are hard to eradicate, requiring almost Herculean reprogramming. As difficult as it is, these patterns may endure for generations.

This book was written from the viewpoint of who I was at the time I was living it, with all the blindness and frailties of an unguided youth. Looking back at my life now, from the serene vista of a sixty-five-year-old, I wryly shake my head, bewildered at the choices of my puppy years. The lures of the world can be deceiving to the unwary. I was very sure of my answers and certain in my ignorance.

As much as I would like to come off as the superheroine of my own story—the wind blowing my red cape and glossy hair back as I assume the victor's stance—I'm afraid the truth is very different. I have never been one of those strong, fierce women that I have wistfully admired. My fears too often made my decisions for me. I compromised my agency and autonomy for the known, seemingly safe limitations of a bondage that ultimately came close to destroying me.

There have been days when, angry and discouraged, I have accusingly looked into the mirror and thought, *whose idea was it to have me come here and deal with this crap?* Of course, it was my own decision. I signed off on it!

Years ago, there was a Far Side cartoon that really hit home for me. In the cartoon, I can almost picture myself as one of the fat, furry lemmings in a crowd standing on a cliff, looking over the edge into a vast, bottomless pit. I'm the short, excitable lemming in the back of the crowd, loudly yelling, "Ooh! Me, first! I wanna go first! Yee Haw!" Sometimes, I have wondered if my coming here wasn't so much an act of faith in Father's Plan as it was an act of stupid optimism about my own abilities.

Although I have accomplished many important things in my life, I have learned much more from my failures, my tragedies, and my disappointments. Unhappiness, like an electric cattle prod, really got my attention! I can only surmise that good and bad times are both necessary for a life of profound growth.

One thing I've discovered is that we all have different areas of our lives that we may keep separate from others. We have a public self, a private self... and we have a secret self. Our public self is what everyone else sees. Sometimes, this public self wears a socially acceptable mask, which can work quite well *'cause no one needs to know all our business.* Our private self is who we are with our family members and very close friends. Our secret self is who we know we are inside—our deepest thoughts and feelings, our shame, things we would rarely, if ever, reveal to others. But we are only as sick as our secrets.

The shame from some of my past experiences was so overwhelming that, for years, I couldn't stand it. So, I drove them from my consciousness. I kept the memories of the bad things I had done and things that were done to me hidden even from myself. I did my best to pretend that none of it ever happened. But deep inside, I had no peace. Occasionally, something would get dredged up, like muck and dead things from a sewer, and I would fall into a deep hole. So, I *had* to heal it. And there was a lot to heal. This has been my life's journey.

I've since learned that it takes strong souls to face their shame. It takes even stronger souls to realistically assess their own flaws and imperfections... and not hate themselves. I'm not that strong. I hate being human. I hate making mistakes. I hate the messiness of it. I cringe often when I look back on my life. *What the heck was I thinking? How was that a good idea? I must have been brain-dead to do that!*

I have sinned, it seems, infinitely. And at the time I sinned, I wasn't sorry. I knew it was wrong, but I chose to do it anyway. I sinned so much that I stopped believing I could ever be worthy enough to return and ask for forgiveness.

So, why write a book, laying bare my past: my sins, my regrets, my shame, my flaws, and my weaknesses? Because of my deep love for you, dear reader. Because I have learned that no matter who or where you are, mercy and forgiveness know no boundaries. No matter how heavy your sins may be, what mistakes you may have made—as can be seen in my life's story—His arms are outstretched wide to receive you Home.

In my many wanderings on strange roads, far from my Father's side, I had become lost. But I realize now that I was not lost to Him. The hope I wish to give you is the recollection that no one is lost to Him. He is eternally reaching out to us. What matters is that we are reaching back.

We are fellow travelers. Let us journey together, hopefully Home. But, as you read my story, be warned: I am the prodigal daughter, including all the iniquity that went with it. I was the rebel, the disaffected, and the offended—the hurt child who was bewildered by life's roll of the dice. For certain, I was the lamb who was lost and then found. But I cannot rest, for

I know there are many other lost lambs who, once like me, feel they are forever lost in the thorns and brambles of exile in the wilderness. My point is, if I could learn how to heed the voice of the Shepherd and follow Him Home, I know you can, too.

It is your choice to make. If the story of my journey can help you, dear reader, as you wander on strange roads as I once did, I will gladly risk what I have to bring you home.

What Level of Worth Are You?

"I asked a Burmese why women, after centuries of following their men, now walked ahead. He said there were many unexploded land mines since the war."
—Raymond Mueller

Hawaii is a beautiful, idyllic place of white sand beaches, year-round sunshine, and green grottos where fern branches hang down enticingly, swaying softly in the breeze like green lace curtains. Many people dream about visiting or living in Hawaii.

Not me. I don't care if I ever go back.

It was in Hawaii that I was raised to believe that certain segments of the population were more important than others and that their needs far outweighed anyone else's. The choices were simple: you could either be miserable or accept this fact–and maybe you could even learn how to get what you needed. Maybe.

Always living on or near military bases, I quickly absorbed the concept of hierarchy. It was apparent that some people were simply more important, more gifted, or more intelligent—I did not know. But they surely deserved more respect, for others showed them with their snaps to attention and salutes. Even as a child, I could tell rank when I saw it from miles away.

In the world, I was told it was a new day. Women could do whatever they wanted now. When I told my elementary school teacher, during career day, that I wanted to be a housewife, her face twisted in stark disappointment, and I somehow knew that wasn't a good enough dream. It was the sixties now, after all. Women were working outside the home, and the sky was supposed to be the limit.

So, I shoved that embarrassing dream of being a mom and a housewife deep down. Then, I set off to find answers to please her like I tried to please everyone else in my little world. But in my home and my reality, there was another hierarchy. As a young female, I was not to speak or want for myself.

One day, as a fifth grader, I walked in on my mother washing my father's clothes. Mom was a pretty Chinese woman with deep brown eyes and short black hair, styled like Jackie Kennedy. She was a serious woman, and whatever she did, she gave it her best effort.

On this day, I watched her silently from the doorway as she gingerly put Dad's underwear into the washing machine. She used just her thumb and forefinger inside of yellow, industrial Playtex gloves, trying to touch as little of the material of his things as possible, her pretty face scrunched up in resigned disgust.

If I had known then what I came to know later, I would have told her to use tongs.

Mom was a secretary for the US Army at Schofield Barracks. She never made much money, but she was the one who kept the lights on in the house and food on the table. She could pinch a penny till it screamed, and my older brother and I never lacked for any necessities.

My father was living off his military retirement check, which didn't stretch too far. As he bounced around from one job to another, usually as a security guard, arguments about money escalated between my parents. Mom couldn't depend on her husband to provide for the family, and all their relatives knew about it. Harsh words forced our huge family to take sides.

Everyone, it seemed, had a very loud opinion. I felt ashamed and scared. *Would I still have a home? What would happen to me?*

These arguments only intensified my mother's sadness, and I hated it when she was sad. We'd been told since we came into her home that Mom had adopted my older brother and me from different homes because she'd been heartbroken about losing two children, and the doctors said she couldn't have any more. I was born in 1959 in Honolulu, Hawaii, on the island of Oahu. I would find out later that my birth mother had been half-Hawaiian, half-Japanese. At eighteen, she placed me for adoption before I was born. I would also discover that my biological father was a Caucasian Navy man stationed at Pearl Harbor. He was already married, with a wife and family back in the mainland United States.

My adopted parents and their family were all second or third-generation Chinese Americans, except for the occasional *haoles* (Hawaiian word for white people or strangers) that married into the family. Adoptive parents in that era were taught to explain their child's adoption to them in a healthy way instead of lying about it. They were advised to share the pain of not being able to have children and how happy they were to have us.

But these stories my mom told me didn't make me feel wanted. Instead, I felt indebted to my parents for taking me in, giving me a home, and providing for me. I felt I shouldn't complain about anything, that I should be grateful, quiet, and not take up too much space. I was fiercely protective of my mother and instinctively knew that my father was behaving badly, even though I didn't know the whole story.

My father had some redeeming qualities. He would take us to the beach to play, and he tried to teach me to surf when I was very young, but I didn't yet know how to swim. He liked to run out to the bakery on Sunday mornings to get sumptuous, fresh-baked pastries to share. Afterward, my parents would drop my brother and me off at the local Congregational church to attend services without them.

I fancied myself a fashionista as a little girl and dressed for church in my prettiest dresses, often hand-me-downs from family. Since I was a quarter Japanese, a quarter Hawaiian, and half white, I had a bit of olive to my skin and brown eyes. I wore my black hair long and Hawaiian curly, which contrasted nicely with the bright, flowery fabrics.

I liked being in church. It was nice and quiet there. Something spoke to me there, though I didn't yet understand that feeling because I rarely felt it anywhere else. Eventually, I learned what it was called. *Peace.*

My parents quit dropping us off at church when things in our house became too tense, and bullies at school squeezed the very joy from my cells. My mother was a beaten-down woman, wearing her polyester pantsuit like a medieval chastity belt, trying to keep my father's filthiness away from her. He was gambling with the few dollars he had and would save up to take trips to Vegas, whether we were eating or not.

One day after school, I was the one to answer the phone when it rang.

"Hi, little girl. Is your daddy home?"

"He's not home," I said truthfully, holding myself steady so my voice wouldn't tremble.

"He's not?" He paused as if he didn't believe me. My stomach dropped, and I began to sweat. A strange and terrible tension filled the line. Finally, the gruff man spoke.

"Well, let him know that we're going to come and *visit* him," he said, his voice filled with menace. "Tell him that his old friends from Vegas are going to come visit him. Maybe he'll go with us on an ocean boat ride."

I hung up the phone, and now I couldn't control the trembling. When Dad found out, I knew he'd either have to look over his shoulder every moment again or go after Mom for money. One night, he got attacked during his job as a security guard. I never heard the whole story, but I heard enough. I decided I would never gamble with money. And while I never became the gambler my father was, I would certainly come to gamble wildly with other aspects of life.

We also received phone calls night and day from other women, and Dad would come home with "gifts" like homemade cakes and cookies, with no good explanation as to where they came from. Divorce was out of the question in our family. Of all the aunts on both sides of my parents' families, only one of my aunts ever divorced her husband. Even when my mother was covered in black and blue marks, she would not leave him. She didn't think she could.

Around the time I turned twelve, something shifted in the dynamics of my family. My father started to look at me differently. I had no words to describe the discomfort I felt when he stared at me—which was often. I had no clue what he was thinking when he looked at me like that. Sometimes, my father, in front of my mother, would stroke my face, neck, shoulders, and my upper arms, and make comments about my appearance. "You're getting so pretty," he would say with a bright, excited look in his eyes. "You're really growing up."

Mom watched us in silence. In fact, everyone was expected to ignore it and pretend it never happened. *Why doesn't my mom stop him?* I wanted to scream. I was hurt and beyond furious that she didn't protect me, but I shoved the hurt and anger deep down inside and blamed myself. I came to understand very well that men do what they want.

As things got worse with my dad, I realized, from conversations in the P.E. locker room, where girls talked about these things, that my father was interested in me sexually. Yet my mom never said a word to stop him when he made these advances toward me. I had been taught I couldn't say no to him—he was our dad!

I was so distressed that I would lock myself in my room when I came home from school and stay there for hours. I began to pray on my own for the first time, asking for guidance. I didn't come out of my room to even use the bathroom until after Dad left for his security job. It was worse when he didn't have a job.

When the Jehovah's Witnesses came to our house, proselytizing, I seized the opportunity to attend their church. I begged my mom to let me go with them. I longed for that feeling when the world slowed down, when what was real became unreal, and what seemed unreal was the biggest truth of all. It continued to be the only place I felt safe.

I also hoped to tell someone, anyone—what was happening in our home. I was desperate to find a way to make my father leave me alone. I hoped God would help me because no one else was protecting me. I never told anyone at the church what was happening in my house. Like my mother, I was blindly loyal to my family. I couldn't tell anyone, only God. I devotedly studied my bible and prayed, but the situation at home continued.

I became depressed and hopeless because no help or answers came. Feeling desperate, I began to feel ambivalent about God. Even though I felt too small and weak, I thought I would have to take on this whole big world by myself. Years later, a profound miracle happened that would let me know there was a God who was lovingly mindful of me. Until then, however, I felt alone and had to do whatever it would take to survive.

So, in the meantime, I gave up any dream having to do with being a housewife—or unhappy wife—as they seemed synonymous. Somehow, I would find the elusive peace I'd only felt a few times in my life, and somehow, I knew that involved getting away from this "paradise."

And this I vowed: I would never live my mother's life.

CHAPTER 1:

Blood in the Water and Thirst in the Desert

"What lies behind us and what lies before us are tiny matters compared to what lies within us."
—Ralph Waldo Emerson

The year Elvis Presley died, people around the world mourned, but the news rocked the islands with the force of a category-five hurricane. Hawaiians had always felt a special connection with Elvis, not only because he had filmed three of his movies in the islands, *Blue Hawaii, Girls, Girls, Girls,* and *Paradise Hawaiian Style*, but because Hawaiians are culturally very musical people who related to his style of singing.

I had grown up in hula classes, learning to dance to several Elvis songs. All the islands were in mourning. Everyone was broken-hearted because he was a part of our *Ohana*. He was our family. Despite my love for Elvis, I couldn't wait to get off the islands and away. Somehow, I knew that Elvis might be *Ohana*, but over the last three years, I knew Hawaii was not my home.

"Oh my God, it's so beautiful!" my dad's friends exclaimed when they came to our area of Hawaii. Both men looked at me. "You are so lucky to live here!" One thing I noticed as they came inside our humble home for a dinner my mother slaved over was that no one talked about the fact that every other season or so, there was blood in the water.

It didn't matter that it didn't happen every day or week or month—our island was surrounded by sharks whose lethal attacks were downplayed by the media. Why couldn't anyone see that I was swimming in shark-infested waters? By the summer after my freshman year of high school, I realized safety was an illusion. I came to believe that love and acceptance were for other people, not me.

Maybe I could become enough, said the constant babble in my head. *Maybe if I worked hard to be good, smarter, prettier, dance the hula better, etc., I could find a friend. I could find safety.* These feelings of inadequacy sent me on a hero's quest to improve myself by focusing on getting as much of an education as I could–both formal and informal education—by reading as many books as possible. I devoured books.

The good news for me was that without long-standing friendships, I had no real peers to experience pressure from. Within a month of starting my sophomore year of high school, I became determined to do things my own way and make my own decisions. When I made a choice, it was truly *my* choice, free from fears of what other people thought of me. That determination became both my superpower and my kryptonite.

Despite my hunger for education, a few months later, when I was fifteen years old, I came home and locked myself in my room until Mom finished her workday.

"Mom, I'm not going back to school. My decision is final."

She looked at me with wide eyes. Women weren't supposed to want anything outside the norm. Yet she knew I was fiercely stubborn and independent. Fortunately, she arranged with the school to have a tutor come to the house once a week to give lessons so I could finish out the school year at home. I completed my sophomore year coursework, then took classes at a local gray concrete community building with no air conditioning to prepare to take my GED.

At not quite sixteen, I was the only minor taking the class, so I studied while waiting a few more months. On my birthday, I went in, took the test, and passed. Hawaii recognized the GED as equivalent to a high school degree, so my high school issued me a diploma, and I graduated a year earlier than my classmates. Now, it was time to get a job so I could avoid my father.

I worked part-time at a donut shop in downtown Honolulu, catching the bus back and forth from my home. At the shop, I met another sixteen-year-old, a boy called Dave. He was Caucasian, with brown hair and interesting blue eyes. He seemed wise, like he somehow knew much more of the world than I did. We hit it off with our mutual sense of humor and love of books, and we started dating. My first boyfriend! Dave drove an old junker car and worked an earlier shift than I did, starting at 4:00 a.m. to help make the donuts. I didn't start my shift until a couple of hours before he got off work, but I lived for those hours of overlap. I was hungry for affection.

Although I was terrific at customer service and building rapport with · customers, I couldn't develop rapport with my boss, an old, creepy, fat guy with hair coming out of his nostrils and spilling over to mix with his gray mustache and beard. I didn't judge his looks but his behavior.

My boss, who worked at the shop every day, would often touch me whenever I had to walk past him to get to the counter. I cringed when he touched my waist, brushed his hand down my back, or grabbed my upper arm for no discernible reason. Like I was taught at home, I ignored him, smiled to keep the peace, and did my job. If it had been a coworker, I'd never put up with it, but it was the hierarchy again.

My boss grew irritated with me for ignoring his advances. One day, when no customers or employees were in the shop but the two of us, he suddenly grabbed my upper arm in his huge hand. This time, he squeezed it for almost ten seconds, his fingers clenching so hard that I gasped and screamed, crying out from the overwhelming pain and trying to get away.

I knew that look in his eyes; he wasn't joking around. He was enjoying a deliberate act of causing pain. I almost fell to the floor at the sheer violence of it. As I stared up at him in shock, he just smiled. Suddenly, he relinquished me, started whistling a tune, and walked away, pretending nothing had happened.

I dried my tears, worked my shift, and held in my pain and tears until I cried quietly to myself as I took the bus home. In my bathroom mirror, the evidence of his violence was apparent in the dark red and black bruising. While I didn't tell my parents, I showed Dave, and then I quit my job. I was sick of terrible men. I went back to the donut shop only one more time to collect my last paycheck, accompanied by Dave. I will never forget the frightened look on my boss's face, worried that Dave would hit him. Dave didn't, but he quit his job afterward in his outrage for me. Had I found solidarity?

At almost seventeen years old, I was stunned by a question: how does someone graduate high school, and suddenly, magically, become transformed into an adult?

I didn't feel like an adult. I was still looking for someone to protect me, and I was grateful for Dave. I felt incapable of taking care of myself—anxious, alone, and waiting for the next bad thing to happen. Dave was also looking for a better life. We decided to marry when we were both seventeen. Although Dave's parents were all for it, Mom wouldn't give her permission at first. *You can't say no! He's my ticket out of here!*

That's when I threatened her with, "Mom, I will never see or speak to you again if you don't!"

Her face crumpled. I felt bad about speaking to her like that, but I couldn't continue to live my life as it was. Every aspect of my world appeared dangerous except Dave.

Dave enlisted in the Air Force, and a month later, finally with both parents' blessings, Dave and I married. We had a one-night honeymoon at a cheap hotel in downtown Honolulu and were happy to have been able to afford it. We were so broke, we ordered fast food, took it to our hotel room and cuddled and watched television. We were just so happy to be together. I was hopeful that I could heal, become stronger, and put the past behind me.

My brand-new husband left for boot camp shortly afterward, and I continued to live with my parents in Hawaii. I avoided my father and waited for Dave to finish his six-week basic training so we could begin our lives together in sheer bliss.

The moment my husband finished boot camp, I finally left the Islands. I flew to join Dave for his advanced training on the mainland USA at Lackland Air Force Base in San Antonio, Texas.

Goodbye and good riddance, Hawaii!

$\cdots\bullet\cdots$

George Carlin once said, "Here's all you need to know about men and women: women are crazy, men are stupid. And the main reason women are crazy is that men are stupid."

One morning, I woke up in Spangdahlem Air Base in West Germany. Joy rushed through me. I was the happiest I'd ever been in my life, even though we had very little. Dave had already left for work, and it was peaceful in our little apartment all day.

After Dave finished his advanced training as an MP (Military Policeman), we were sent to our first assignment overseas. It was a great adventure, and we lived in base guest housing for a while until we found a small rental apartment off-base. It was cold and strange in Germany, and I didn't speak one word of the language or know the customs. Still, I was okay with staying indoors because my clothes from Hawaii didn't keep me warm in German winters. Dave's salary was so small that it took some time to save up for a coat of my own after paying for food and rent, plus other bills.

That didn't matter. I had never seen snow before, and I watched it fall softly over the rooftops. It was breathtakingly beautiful. Plus, I was experiencing my secret, private dream, keeping everything clean, making dinner for my new husband, and being a housewife. I even hand-washed his clothes in the shower in a bucket, hanging his uniforms to dry before proudly ironing and starching them.

The apartment was tiny, with one tiny bedroom, one tiny bathroom, and a little kitchenette to clean, and that was it. It left a lot of time to read books.

Dave loved spy novels by Robert Ludlum, such as *The Bourne Identity*, and he had a whole collection of paperbacks that I gradually worked my way through, enjoying them very much. We didn't have a television, but it didn't matter because all the programs were in German, anyway.

One day, as I finished a story, closing the back cover for the last time, I experienced a sudden memory, all too real, of my father touching me and my efforts to avoid him. It left me shaking and trembling, nauseated and angry. In the quiet of the apartment, it happened again the next day and the next.

These flashbacks were very intrusive and randomly appeared with no warning. I hated that they felt so real, as I suffered all the emotions as if it was happening *now*. Each time, they triggered overwhelming feelings of panic, anxiety, and fear, followed by self-blame, self-loathing, and grief deeper than I'd ever felt before.

But even in my suffering, there was mercy. To survive, my mind began to cloud over, and I forgot what my dad had done to me. Each time after, God seemed to miraculously help me forget what was too painful for my consciousness to handle.

I didn't tell Dave about the flashbacks. I just wanted to forget. It was disconcerting to me that once I had reached a safe haven with Dave and relaxed, these tamped-down memories rose, unbidden, to the surface.

Several weeks later, I started throwing up and feeling nauseous. Dave took me to the base clinic. I didn't think I was pregnant because I was on the pill. When the doctor told me my pregnancy test came back positive, I was in disbelief. I stared at him with wide eyes. I didn't know how I felt other than scared. Dave was standing when the doctor told us the news, and he almost fainted. It absolutely shocked him. He wobbled and then caught himself, having to grab the wall for support.

He sat. I sat. Of course, I was keeping the baby, but I knew I wasn't ready to be a mother. *I can't even take care of and support myself. How will I be able to take care of a baby?* While it was smart for us to have children while Dave was in the military due to the free medical care, we hadn't expected to face this event for another year or two.

Several months later, my daughter, Danni, was born. She was the most beautiful, perfect baby I had ever seen. I loved all babies and thought they were all gorgeous, but I could not believe that this beautiful angel had been created by my body! I was so amazed and thankful that she was healthy, with five fingers on each tiny hand and five toes on each tiny foot.

In the privacy of my shower, however, I could not contain my incessant crying. I felt guilty for bringing this child into the world. I grieved because I knew that this exquisite, immaculate, wonderful child deserved a better mother than me. I did not feel worthy of Danni one whit. As she grew from day to day, then month to month, I was trying to heal myself, but it was so hard.

I prayed that this child would not have the life I'd had. *Please, God*, I pleaded, *let her have a happy life! I will do the best I can, I promise, but my best might not be good enough.* Then, I would sob some more. *I'm sorry, God, that I'm so wounded. How can a broken bird give this child her own wings to fly in the world?*

I didn't know if God was listening, but I prayed anyway. For most of my life, I had no one else but God to talk to about my fears and loneliness. I prayed sporadically, sometimes desperately, but never recognized any answers. *Please help me!* I prayed now. I realized how ironic it was that my parents never role-modeled prayer for me. They were taught it, so they just went through the motions of teaching me—unemotional and dismissive of the words of the Lord's Prayer, ticking off boxes, no faith required.

Dave and I were in Germany for a year when the Air Force moved us again, this time back to the USA, to Kirtland Air Force Base in Albuquerque, New Mexico. Danni was four and a half months old, and I discovered Albuquerque was a nice change of scenery and climate. The desert air in New Mexico was drier than I was used to, but welcome. It was also nice to be back in the States, where most people spoke English.

Shortly after we settled in, I found out I was pregnant again. This time, it didn't trouble me because I felt more confident as a mother after caring for Danni. Besides, Dave and I had talked about having two children and felt that Danni needed a sibling close to her age.

Initially, Dave seemed happy to be with me and Danni and happy at the prospect of being a father again. Within a few months, however, he became emotionally withdrawn and started disappearing. He would hop on his friend's dirt bike to "go on trails" for hours at a time. He seemed happier when he got back, so I didn't mind... too much.

Soon, however, he was gone all day on weekends and after work during the week, supposedly riding the dirt bike. He wouldn't get home till late at night. I started getting frustrated because I felt he was acting immature and selfishly.

Then, one day, when I was nearly seven months pregnant, I discovered he'd sold our family car in order to buy his friend's dirt bike, without discussing it with me. I was stunned. We were a family with one child and another on the way, I was edging nearer to delivery, and we now had only a dirt bike for transportation.

What the heck is going on?

"Dave, we need a car!" I cried indignantly. "How are we supposed to buy groceries or take Danni to the doctor for her immunizations? And the baby, when she comes, for all her checkups? How am I supposed to get to the hospital when I go into labor?"

"I'll pick up food and diapers for you," he said calmly, as if he had it all thought out, "and if we need a car, I can borrow one from one of my friends."

"You had no right to sell the car without asking me!"

"Whatever."

I was at my wit's end. My belly was huge, and my back hurt. I felt tired and nauseous most of the time. It was hard to keep up with Danni. She was an active, bright child with a lively personality, and I enjoyed playing with her, but at this point in the pregnancy, it wore me out. Without a car, I couldn't take her to a park or a pool or a sitter.

I also needed Dave to help me. I was at home by myself all day and most of the night.

"Dave, you're a father now. You can't be off with your friends riding dirt bikes all day and night. Look at me; I'm exhausted! How will I be able to contact you when you're out riding in the desert? Also, what if something happens to you? How will I know? Please don't leave Danni and me alone for so long," I begged, but he continued his near-daily excursions. We had a landline, but that was useless if he was on the trail. I'd begun to suspect he wasn't *always* on the trail, but I was worried most about our almost two-year-old daughter, Danni. She hardly saw her father.

One day, Dave came home from work on the base, and I tried to talk him into picking up a few personal items before heading out again on his dirt bike. We were both in the living room, and Danni was napping in her bedroom.

"Dave, what do I do if I have to go to the hospital?" I asked him again. "What if there's an emergency? What if I go into labor early?" I put my hand on his forearm and looked him in the eyes. "What do I do about Danni if the baby comes and you're not home?"

"Just put her in her bedroom with some food, shut the door, and she'll be fine till I get home," he said flippantly.

"Are you out of your mind?" I cried, and a fire grew inside of me. I screamed at him, "What kind of father says something like that?"

Dave just shrugged his shoulders and walked out the front door. I heard him start up his dirt bike and loudly drive off, the roar of the motor disappearing with him. Over the next week, he continued to leave us alone for very long periods of time. I felt so much shame, thinking something must be wrong with me. But one thing I knew was that Danni didn't deserve this, and neither did our upcoming daughter.

I finally told a new friend I'd met, Shay. When I caught her up on Dave's nefarious behavior, she nodded calmly while listening to me, but her eyes were wide and shocked.

As I watched her face contort in fury, I felt like maybe I wasn't crazy for feeling so frustrated. I took the oddest comfort in seeing her face grow redder and redder and her anger ready to explode.

Shay was not a shrinking violet. We were about the same age but light-years apart in our differing abilities to move through the world. She was an opinionated, fierce, and very confident young woman who had once organized a labor strike at her fast-food job, where all her co-workers had followed her lead, quitting their jobs over management mistreatment. Shay's motto continued to be, "What's right is right, and what isn't is wrong." She didn't put up with any crap. That was not her style.

"I'm so very, very sorry, Jade. It's not safe for you to stay with Dave. You and Danni are welcome to come and stay at my house until you can figure out what you want to do about this... ugh, horrible situation!"

So, Danni and I moved out of my on-base house and in with Shay and her husband, Lukas. Lukas worked with Dave in the military, in the same police unit on the Air Force Base. Initially, we'd had dinner at each other's houses from time to time, but now they wanted nothing to do with Dave. Like angels, they rallied around Danni and me, enclosing us in their protection. Only then did I discover I had more to be protected from than just a negligent husband.

"We wanted to tell you, Jade, but we didn't know how to," Lukas said. "He's been having sex with other women when he's out with his friends. He's been bragging about it to everyone at work."

Dear God. So, finally, I knew the truth! I was shocked but not surprised. I had suspected that something had been going on. I was angry and upset. *I am not putting up with this!* I felt duped. *How can Dave treat his own family like this? What happened to our marriage?* It seemed that Dave didn't want me or his children anymore. He wanted to erase us from his life. *Erase me, okay, but how do you erase your own children?*

Finally, I got a lawyer to help me divorce Dave. It was tough to discover there were sharks everywhere, not just in Hawaii. It seemed my vulnerable situation as an unemployed, single mother with a small child attracted them. I was wounded, and they could smell the blood in the water. I was suddenly a magnet for certain men, some of them even *friends* of my ex-husband! My very obvious pregnancy didn't even deter them. I fended them off, experiencing anxiety through some stalking incidents. Their unwelcome and intrusive efforts to insert themselves into my life made me feel angry, scared, and vulnerable. I felt unsafe all the time.

The realization hit me. I was living my mother's life... and it ticked me off!

Less than a month later, it was my friend, Shay, who held my hand as I gave birth to my second daughter. I called her Shayna. She was just as beautiful as Danni, with brown hair, blue eyes, and a button nose. I didn't know how the three of us were going to make it, but I felt a surge of hope looking at my brand-new angel baby! Somehow, we would manage. I determined I would move mountains for these beautiful girls!

CHAPTER 2:

Moving Mountains, Crossing Seas

"Knowing your own darkness is the best method for dealing with the darknesses of other people."
—Carl Jung

And move mountains, I did. I got a job as a waitress and faced trying to find a babysitter and living in a women's shelter for a time so I could keep my girls safe. In Dave's mind, his daughters were not his problem anymore, and he would do nothing to help unless he was forced. I wasn't living in a "win-lose" situation where there was a good choice or a bad choice. I was living a "lose-lose" situation, where every choice was a bad option. Dave, on the other hand, had his cake and ate it, too. I had to provide for and protect my children by myself, even though it was a struggle to feed the three of us, one meal at a time.

One afternoon, I'd caught the bus after work to go to the sitter so I could take my girls home to the shelter. I had to stop to transfer at a station. I walked through the empty parking lot by some empty truck rigs to where my next bus connection was. As I came around the back of an eighteen-wheeler,

I saw a man sitting in the driver's seat of a big, tall rig, holding a struggling child, a little blond boy about five years old, in his lap.

The little boy was sitting in the man's lap, facing the steering wheel. The child's face was contorted with pain and crying. I stopped walking and glared at the man. He immediately stopped what he was doing and instinctively put his hand over the boy's mouth. Just as quickly, he took his hand off the boy's mouth as if he thought better of it with me as a witness. Then, he grinned a big, fake smile at me. The little boy slumped forward against the steering wheel, helpless and blank-faced, as if he had endured more than he could bear.

I couldn't see everything that was going on inside the truck, but I had a cold, eerie feeling. I stood there, glaring at him to make sure he knew I saw him and that he'd better stop whatever he was doing to make the child cry.

Let him think I'm going to call the cops on him, I thought. *I bet he won't hurt the kid again.*

Seeing that child looking so tortured made me anxious for my own two children. I wracked my brain to think of how to keep them safe when I wasn't around. I had to work to provide for them. I ran to my transfer bus and got on, hurrying to get to my daughters. I got to them safely, but within hours, unable to keep that little boy out of my mind, I realized my problems were more than I could cope with in New Mexico.

With much trepidation, I decided I needed to return to Hawaii, where I was familiar with the people and the area and had relatives who could provide me and my children with at least some protection and support. I was terrified to have to move back in with my parents. I could only pick what I thought was the lesser of two evils. But on my terms this time.

"I need your help, Mom! But I also need you to make sure that Dad is *never* alone with Danni and Shayna."

My mother went dead quiet. I could feel she was wrestling with her emotions. I heard her breathing become erratic over the phone. Her panic was almost tangible, a riptide trying to drag her down to invisible, swirling depths. I felt her pain, as well as my own, as I gripped the phone and waited for her to reply.

You can only be in denial for so long before something rises to the surface and slaps you across the face. Wake up!

Then, I prayed. *Please, God, even though she didn't protect me, let her love for her grandchildren be strong enough to bear this suffering and do the right thing!*

Someone had to break this silence. I realized it was me.

"Mom, you or I or a babysitter needs to be with the girls all the time. We must make sure there is always a responsible adult watching the girls whenever Dad is around them. Do you agree to do that with me?"

"Yes. Yes, I will do that with you. Your father will never be left alone with the girls. I promise."

I broke down and sobbed in sheer relief. "Thank you, Mom." With tears running down my face, my voice wavered as I choked, "I love you, Mom. We'll do this together. We'll keep Danni and Shayna safe."

Within weeks, I was back in Hawaii, in "paradise" again. I needed a really great job.

Mom was ecstatic to see me and her new grandchildren. As I watched her joyfully hug and kiss their faces, I noticed she looked so much older than when I had last seen her three years prior. Her pretty hair had lost its color and grayed, and the lines in her face had deepened and become sharper, worn down from dealing with my father's selfish behaviors. She murmured to me, in private, that he seemed to have committed to a relationship with his current girlfriend. After he finished his job on the swing and night shifts, he spent many nights with her instead of at home. Sad as I should have been for my mother, I only felt relief.

Every day, I got up and watched my dad carefully when he was home. I wasn't afraid of him anymore because I could defend myself, but my children couldn't. I was hypervigilant, and the familiar stress exhausted me, giving me nightmares when I tried to sleep, even when he was gone. It was impossible to relax.

Two months after our arrival and after frequent trips to the mailbox, I realized no more child support checks were being forwarded to me. I contacted the courts, and to my dismay, I found out that Dave had been discharged from the military and had disappeared, leaving no forwarding address.

Years later, I would discover that Dave had remarried and had three more children with his new wife. I wondered how Dave found it so easy to abandon his two daughters. Did he ever wonder if they were hungry? Did he ever wonder if they were being abused? He knew the situation in my home with my dad and how grateful I'd been to leave when we married. Was he ever afraid for his children? Did he care for them? I didn't know. Whatever the case, it was obvious he didn't care *enough*.

Now, in my mother's living room, a feeling of deep betrayal shot through me for a second time, and I wanted to rip that "no support" notice into shreds. *What a jerk!* I thought of a few other choice expletives, then took a few days to wrap my head around it all. I had to go on welfare to feed my babies. Welfare was a stopgap measure, but I knew this path was a dead end. I had to get off of it as soon as possible. The day I signed up at the welfare office, I looked around and saw unhealthy, even generational patterns of dependence.

Determined to make this a temporary solution, I went to work at a popular fast-food joint, but quickly discovered I was going nowhere on slave wages. The costs of babysitting for two children, one still an infant, didn't provide me with any money left over. Plus, I owed my attorney thousands of dollars. He was trying to help me go after Dave for non-existent child support, but I had no idea how I was going to pay for the attorney's enormous fees.

I decided to find a job as a waitress, preferably at night, so that I could take care of my children during the day. *What safe food or beverage place could I walk to at night to support my girls while Mom watches over them? Where can I earn enough money to get out of here as soon as possible?*

CHAPTER 3:

Out of the Frying Pan

M any restaurants and fast-food places, including the Golden Arches, paid a copper salary—nothing to support a family, but my choices were limited. *What should I do?* I applied for a job as a waitress at a bar close to my house, hopeful that I could earn tips on top of a small hourly salary.

On my first day, I stood in the main entrance door of the bar, looking straight across the parking lot to where I remembered clearly, as a child, a man had tried to get me into his car while I was walking home from my elementary school. He said he was lost and "needed my help," but my childhood intuition kicked in, and I ran from him just in time. I never saw him again, but it didn't keep me from reflexively scanning the faces of all the male patrons of the bar on the chance that he might show up. I wondered what I would do to him if I ever saw him again.

Antifreeze in a drink, maybe? Drano or rat poison in a cup of coffee?

Would he recognize me if he saw me again? I doubted it; I wasn't his type anymore—far too old at twenty-two years.

The funny thing at this bar was there wasn't much running around serving food or drinks, even though we served both. Most of the demand and supply at the bar was from older, married men wanting to enjoy sitting at a table with a pretty young girl, talking to her, and buying her drinks. I had stumbled into working at a Korean bar. I didn't even know what that was, at first.

Korean bars, also known as "hostess bars," were named after the bars during the Korean War where the local Korean women would set up places for the American soldiers to drink, eat, relax, and be around women when they had time for some R & R (rest and recreation). There were a *lot* of Korean bars in Hawaii... and there were a lot of married men wanting attention.

I worked as a hostess at the bar, walking around the booths and tables and checking to see if the customers, mostly men, needed a refill on their drinks. We served food at the bar, too, mostly nibbly bits. There was a cook in the back who could whip up most kinds of local Hawaiian delicacies, like an *opihi* seaweed salad, deep-fried tofu fingers in ginger and soy sauce, a hot watercress salad, or even big hot pots of bubbling broth with noodles, beef, and vegetables for a large table.

A lot of married men came there with their girlfriends, or to find a girlfriend. None of my business. The very pretty Japanese owner of the bar had a boyfriend who was also married. He looked like a Filipino Elvis Presley, with his mutton-chop sideburns and flashy clothes. He hung out with her in the back while she kept an eye on her establishment. I didn't think much of him because it seemed to me that he was always asking her for money.

All the hostesses were encouraged by the owner and the manager to dress attractively but not seductively. The look we were to go for was "the girl next door." Not a lot of makeup or fancy clothes. Just clean, lady-like, and presentable.

Many of the men who were regulars at the bar had a certain girl they liked working as a hostess. They often came after work or dinner, rarely with their families, to spend time sitting with a pretty girl. The tips were much better than at my old, hourly fast-food jobs. Some nights, the tips were five times more than I made working at the Golden Arches.

One day, after I'd been working as a hostess for about six months, the bartender with a Fu Manchu mustache flagged me down as I walked back to the station to get a refill for a customer. "Where's Cindy?" he barked. "Her customers are sitting by themselves. That's not good for business!"

The deal at the Korean bar was that the girls would keep the men happy by sitting with them at their table, listening to all their problems or whatever topic they wanted to talk about for the night, serving them drinks, joking with them, and entertaining them so they would relax. The point was to keep them buying drinks and show them a good time so they would want to return, again and again. The bar depended upon a regular clientele. Hostesses were told that if they were smart, they would develop a loyal group of clients who would return to the bar often just to see them.

The tricky part of working as a hostess happened when a lot of your regular customers came in at the same time. You would have to rotate between your customers, being careful not to spend too much time with any one of them. It was taboo to show too much favoritism to any one customer, or the rest of your customers would become furious and leave.

Still, almost all the clientele that came to a Korean bar knew that buying the girls drinks was how the girls earned their living, so they bought drinks for them and tipped them well. Each time a customer bought a hostess a drink, she would get a *nikohana* from the bar, and she would keep the money the customer paid her. A *nikohana* was just plain Coca-Cola or 7 Up, no alcohol, and the bar would not charge her any money for them. We would sometimes lie and say our drinks *did* contain alcohol for new customers who weren't familiar with the ritual, just to keep them happy, but all the regular customers knew there was no alcohol in a *nikohana*. A girl could make more money by drinking a *nikohana* than a drink containing alcohol since she could safely drink more of them and stay witty without getting drunk.

The girls rarely got drunk. In fact, it was looked down upon for a hostess to get drunk. How could she entertain her customers if she was drunk? It was fine if *he* got drunk, but there were rules of integrity. I had even seen experienced Asian hostesses return money to a customer so drunk that he just kept throwing money at her. It was about treating the customer with respect.

Our job was to provide a safe place where the customer could drink and not feel that he would be taken advantage of, although truth be told, sometimes that did happen. If a customer really liked a girl, there were very expensive drinks they could purchase, like a hundred-dollar bottle of champagne, that the girl would split 50/50 with the bar and take home fifty dollars as part of her tips. The sale of alcohol was a money-maker for the bar and its hostesses alike.

This was a whole new world for me. I discovered that there was a longstanding tradition of geishas in the Orient, where it was acceptable for a man to spend time with another woman while his wife stayed at home, raising his kids. The Oriental culture was designed around the assumption that a man was the most important creature on earth, and women were just objects to serve a man's desires. The whole system was designed to cater to the needs of men. Women weren't allowed to have needs of their own—except for when a man allowed her to.

As I began to be more educated about the world, I read and saw how, too often, women were treated like dirt. It took a smart woman to get what she wanted and to create a life she wanted, even when she was treated like chattel. I'd heard of this concept in an old Southern saying of a woman having an "iron hand in a velvet glove," where the woman has convinced the man that he is in charge, even though she is really the one in charge.

I noticed how the most highly skilled hostesses made the men at their tables feel wanted, but they ruled the tables. There were also women not smart enough to be that iron hand in the velvet glove. Although prostitution was not allowed at the bar, the owner couldn't control what the girls did after working hours. Many hostesses found boyfriends with financial benefits. However, the traditional construct of geishas was that they were *not* prostitutes but entertainers and artists, giving a man a romantic experience and an excitement missing from his daily life. Thank goodness, this was different from the goal of a geisha centuries prior, which was to find a patron who would support her and pay all her bills because he wanted an exclusive relationship with her, including sex.

I walked into the bar the next night to hear a loud, angry conversation in Japanese between the bar owner and Ka-chan, the oldest hostess at the bar, who served as the manager when the owner was absent. The owner was so furious that if she could have spit venom, she would have.

Quietly, I asked the bartender, "What's going on?"

"We found out where Cindy was last night when she disappeared." Apparently, Cindy had been under one of the booth tables, giving a customer something not on the menu! Cindy was a Caucasian college student from California, temporarily in Hawaii on vacation. This job—and apparently her extra-curricular activities at the bar paid for her vacation expenses. Vacation over.

Since Cindy was no longer working at the bar, some of the male customers who had been Cindy's clients openly laughed and bragged about receiving "special favors" from her. Cindy was the first white girl the owner had hired, and she was furious that Cindy had turned her bar into a brothel. All the other hostesses were local girls—Japanese, Chinese, Hawaiian, or *hapa haole* (mixed race, half-white) like me. The owner complained that white girls had no concept of what a Korean bar was. She flatly refused to hire another one.

I heard that other Korean bars on the island hired the Caucasian wives of US military soldiers who were stationed in the islands. We had Navy, Marine, Army, Air Force, and Coast Guard military personnel and their families living on the island. One soldier, a social acquaintance of mine, freely admitted his wife worked at a Korean bar. He bragged that one night, she came home with a brand-new television that a customer at the bar had bought for her. The woman's husband thought it was the greatest thing ever! I was astonished but kept my mouth shut and smiled politely.

I wondered why any man would want his wife to work in a Korean bar when he had a good job and was able to support her. I came to realize this guy was benefiting from the money his wife made and was all for it.

One thing I knew was if I had had a more doable option, I would not have chosen to work in a Korean bar. In my book, it was only one step above welfare and another dead end. I saw older hostesses who had wasted their youth working in the bar until they were old and had only a few loyal customers left.

If a girl is smart, I thought, *she'll save her money while she is young to better her life.* It took months and months, but I finally caught up on the financial ruin Dave had put us in, and I hoped to save for that better life for me and my daughters.

Then, one night, six months after Cindy was fired, I snuck out the back to walk home in the dark after the bar closed. A group of young male patrons who had been at the Korean bar that night drove past me, hollering and catcalling me. I ignored them, turned quickly into a side street, and walked swiftly down several other streets, turning in different directions in a roundabout way to lose them. It felt all too familiar, that high-adrenaline feeling of being stalked and followed—the same feeling I'd had as a child. Although I was an adult now, I felt powerless against a group of men in that heightened situation.

Now my secret is out! I walked home each night as I still couldn't afford a car, but it was obviously not safe for me to work at the bar anymore. I couldn't take a chance on being attacked or having a man follow me home.

Fortunately, over the past several months, I had been working on getting another job. Having finally paid off my attorney, I was able to quit the bar the next day. Then, I immediately enlisted in the United States Army. I had to make good use of my time to get financially stable enough to pull my kids out of my parents' home. The clock was ticking.

CHAPTER 4

OD Green is the New Black

"Just because nobody complains doesn't mean all parachutes are perfect."
—Benny Hill

"This place smells like a frickin' whorehouse!" muttered Drill Sergeant Reece, shaking his head as he stalked into the barracks. He laser-locked his mean, brown eyes on each of us females as he strode down the length of the room. We all stood stiffly at attention in a line in front of our bunk beds, desperately hoping to blend in and be invisible. At least, that was what I was trying to do. We were all dressed in our BDUs (battle dress uniforms), which had a printed pattern of mostly OD (olive drab) green.

Even though I was still petrified, I chuckled inwardly at the sight. Compared to the Korean bar I had just come from, we women looked like short, squat men.

Welcome to Fort Jackson, Columbia, South Carolina! Ronald Reagan was the President of the United States of America. I was getting a massive dose of patriotism, and it was my first week in Boot Camp... that lovely time in a new female soldier's life where they pamper you and treat you like you're God's gift to men.

Not!

I was a member of an all-female platoon, and in addition to Drill Sergeant Reece, we also reported to Drill Sergeant Willis at Tank Hill, otherwise known as Tank Hell.

Drill Sergeant Reece was all lean muscle, dark hair, and a cruel gaze. Whenever I picture Satan in my head, he looks just like Drill Sergeant Reece. Having finished his Jungle Expert training—whatever that was—in Panama the month before, it was clear he was grieving the loss of his male trainees.

"I can't stand you females," he groused. "I can't wait for you all to finish and get the hell outta here so I can get me some real soldiers." From his words, his tone of voice, and his actions, it was quite clear he *hated* us. Nevertheless, orders were orders. He was here to do a job.

Drill Sergeant Willis, on the other hand, was a tall, quiet man with smoldering violence in his visage. Picture Clint Eastwood in *Dirty Harry. So, do you feel lucky, punk? Well, do ya?* Willis mostly hovered in the background and didn't have to do much to keep us female trainees in line, if only because we were already scared to death of Drill Sergeant Reece. So, unlucky punk that I was, I got both Satan and Dirty Harry for drill sergeants. I was constantly looking for a rock to crawl under whenever I saw either of them walking my way.

On the first day of boot camp, Drill Sergeant Reece took the only obvious lesbian in the platoon, Marshall, and made her squad leader. She looked the most masculine of all of us, so I guess he felt confident in her ability to help run things. The rest of us females in the platoon were frilly little feminine things, a fact that he looked very sad about. He named our platoon "Bushmasters," after a South American snake that he'd probably killed with a knife and eaten raw in Panama.

Drill Sergeant Reece would put the whole platoon in the plank position you are in to do push-ups, but he would just *leave* us with arms extended, the palms of our hands blistering on the hot pavement and gravel in the scorching South Carolina sun. All the while, he would regale us with stories of the good ol' days when he had men for trainees.

He told us about the times he made his male trainees take all the furniture out of the barracks: metal bunk beds, tall metal double lockers, footlockers, chairs, and the desk from his office, plus everything else in the barracks, and set them up on the grass outside in the exact positions they had been in the barracks. He would then go around with a ruler and measure everything so that he knew, for sure, they were in the same position as they were inside, to the inch. Once he was satisfied that it was perfect, he would make his trainees move everything back into the barracks, in exactly the same positions they were in originally. The man just liked to screw with his trainees. This hazing was a tradition he made every platoon he trained go through—until he got to us females. He seemed quite unhappy that he couldn't make our female platoon do the same.

"Weak, weak, weak!" he'd say. "You're all weak!"

There were male platoons in our company, called Company C, training with other drill sergeants, but no fraternization was allowed between males and females during boot camp. Despite this, a girl from another platoon was caught having sex with a male trainee in an empty garbage dumpster. Both were put on KP duty (kitchen patrol or kitchen police) in separate kitchens, peeling potatoes and performing other duties for the next two weeks of boot camp, in addition to their regular duties. The joke in the military was that KP really stood for "Keep Peeling."

One day, my platoon and I were trained on gas masks. Oh, what joy, learning how to fit the masks to our faces before being exposed to the actual gas itself. I lined up with the other gals, ready to go into a gas-filled tent, take off my mask, and recite my social security number before being let out of the tent. We all had to sign off that we'd successfully completed this part of the training.

When it was my turn, I entered the tent, took off my mask, and gasped. Suddenly, I couldn't talk. I couldn't even catch my breath. My inability to recite my social security number irritated the proctor in the tent, and through his own mask, he ordered me to the back of the line without being allowed to put my mask back on. I became frantic, with my eyes bulging and my throat burning, because I couldn't get any air into my lungs. My eyes teared up so badly, I couldn't see. Tears and snot dripped down my face, and my mouth dripped saliva in my struggle to breathe.

I tried to run out of the tent, but the proctor decided to make an example of me. He grabbed the back of my collar and yanked me back into the tent. Then, he sent me to the end of the line again! My panic for air only increased. *I am going to die!*

Suddenly, Drill Sergeant Reece, in his gas mask, was in front of me, checking my helmet for my name written on masking tape on the front, like all the trainees.

"Are you my trainee?" he yelled through the mask.

I couldn't answer him. I was incapable of talking or breathing.

Recognizing my name, Reece grabbed me by the front collar of my BDUs and threw me unceremoniously out of the tent. I landed on my butt and rolled over. I spent the next thirty minutes throwing up in the grass with snot, tears, and sweat running down my face and body. Not pretty. But I could breathe. I would live... until next time. I was never so grateful as when I passed that particular test.

Two weeks later, we were at the firing range. The trainees at the front of the lines were in a prone position with their M16A1 rifles, getting ready to fire at their targets. Drill Sergeant Reece and Drill Sergeant Willis were walking among the trainees who were on their bellies on the ground, checking to see if we were in the correct position to fire our weapons.

Reece marched over to me as I was lying on the ground and kicked me several times with his combat boots until I managed to get in the "proper" prone position. *Damn, that hurts!* Just another day in paradise!

To everyone's surprise, including mine, I became a good shot. Even Drill Sergeant Reece was impressed. He complimented me on qualifying as an expert shot and had a new nickname for me: Hawkeye. Satan even grudgingly admitted that I had exceeded his expectations for a female trainee.

By week four, my platoon members noticed that Drill Sergeant Reece and Drill Sergeant Willis always had a chaw of tobacco in their mouths. We decided that we were going to try chewing tobacco, too.

One day soon after, Drill Sergeant Reece had our squad leader, Marshall, put us in formation, only to discover that his whole platoon of frilly, feminine trainees had chewing tobacco in their mouths. We were all supposed to be looking straight ahead, but I couldn't help but quickly glance over to see his reaction. It was clear he couldn't believe it. He even did a double take, and I could have sworn he got misty-eyed.

Moments later, he bragged to another passing drill sergeant of lesser female trainees,

"You see my Bushmasters; they're tough!"

I used a chewing tobacco called Levi Garrett for the rest of boot camp, and I swallowed, not spit. It made me feel a little dizzy sometimes, but I felt I had to live up to the elite standards of the Bushmasters!

The girls bonded as a platoon as the weeks went by. One day, when our platoon was out on a run in full gear with our heavy, awkward rucksacks, one of the female trainees, Farrow, gave up and stopped running. Our squad leader, Marshall, went back and got her. The next thing I knew, she was running, carrying both her own and the other girl's rucksack, even as she dragged Farrow by her arm the rest of the way. We all had to complete the run, or the whole platoon would be in trouble. Trailing in last with Farrow, Marshall threw Farrow's rucksack on the ground and disgustedly dogged her out for letting the platoon down.

"You need to get straight and stop shamming, Farrow! I'm not hauling your butt around anymore!"

The next morning, Farrow didn't show up for formation with the rest of us. Drill Sergeant Reece went looking for her. *Holy crap!* He told us later that he had found her sitting on her bunk with an open can of Brasso, a liquid used to polish metal, next to her. He said she had tried to drink it as a suicide attempt, which Farrow privately denied to the rest of us.

Drill Sergeant Reece kicked her out of the Army and sent her home, which was probably for the best. I couldn't believe I was hanging in there on certain days. But while I did not seek out attention when my drill sergeants were coming, I no longer completely cowered.

Physical Training (PT) was a major part of our days. We would exercise every morning, push-ups and sit-ups, followed by a run of several miles in formation, singing military cadence songs, also known as "Jody calls." These Jody calls not only helped us stay in step while running or marching but served to take our minds off the pain or tiredness in our bodies. They motivated us to run farther and train harder—and sometimes, were even a bit fun. We felt like a team.

I remember the runs, or rather crawls, we did up and down and all through the sand dunes called Little Egypt on Fort Jackson, South Carolina. It killed me. *I never want to run in the sand again.*

It didn't matter. We had to run everywhere we went, in every weather, even to the chow hall. We weren't allowed to walk anywhere; we had to keep running as part of our physical conditioning. We were made to drop and do push-ups by any drill sergeant who might see us walking. When our drill sergeant was told about it, he dropped us for additional pushups—or worse. You never wanted to find out what *worse* was! It was guaranteed to ruin your day, maybe even your week.

Finally, it was graduation day for whoever in the platoon had survived. Our drill sergeants had us in formation for the last time. Drill Sergeant Reece looked us over and reminisced about how we'd all changed since arriving at Fort Jackson. He remarked, surprised, to Drill Sergeant Willis, "Hey, look. Parker made it!"

He probably would have given me a zero chance of making it to graduation on day one, but here I was at the end, confident and fit with my platoon, having hung in there.

I speculated that Drill Sergeant Reece was proud of us. I thought Drill Sergeant Willis was, too, but it was hard to tell. He still never talked much. I was surprised to see Drill Sergeant Reece smile a lot on our graduation day. But it wasn't in pride. He had a lot to look forward to, bragging that he was getting male trainees for his next cycle of boot camp.

I could almost hear the metal bunk beds being dragged across the barracks floor.

••●••

After I finished boot camp, I was transferred to another location in Fort Jackson called Old Hollywood and New Hollywood, where I did my Advanced Individual Training (AIT). Here, I trained for the job I would perform in the Army. My military occupational specialty (MOS) was a 71 Lima, Administrative Specialist. I was basically a clerk/typist, like the character Radar on the television series *MASH*.

The joke among 71 Limas was that it wasn't wise for anyone to get on our bad side. We had the power to type up transfer papers and have our enemies reassigned to Greenland. Yup. It's very cold and dark there for much of the year. For fun, you could visit the Greenland Ice Sheet.

In AIT, I was delighted to find that we had more freedom. We could get weekend passes to leave Fort Jackson and go off-post to the city of Columbia. We could eat in restaurants, go shopping, get a hotel room, etc., just as long as we were back for formation and roll-call bright and early on Monday mornings, ready to go for a run. We could even hang out with and date members of the opposite sex. A lot of people took advantage of this new freedom.

The whole Army unit had formation out on the grounds in front of our barracks every morning, Monday through Friday. That's where I first saw Kyle. I thought he was cute, but I wasn't trying to hook up with anyone. I was serious about my job. I was working to be a good provider for my children back in Hawaii. Still, sometimes I would go on weekend passes with friends off-post, and we would get a room as a group and inexpensively have fun. I ran into Kyle at a hotel one weekend, where he was crashing with some friends. I said, "Hi," and walked away to go to my room. I was pleased when he chased me down the hallway.

"Jade, Jade, Jade! Hey, slow down. Do you want to get something to eat?"

He was trying to get into my pants, working overtime on being charming, and convinced me to hang out with him. We had a nice dinner and talked about anything and everything. Then, we went back to my room to talk some more and watch television. My roommates for the weekend must have been getting some action because nobody disturbed us.

Just like typical twenty-somethings do on first dates, we asked each other all kinds of personal questions to get to know one another. Kyle told me he was a half-brother to a famous singer in a very popular heavy metal band. He also told me that Kyle wasn't his real name and that he had enlisted in the Army using a different name to get out of California for a while.

I was skeptical of his story, but he insisted he was telling me the truth. He looked like this famous recording artist's twin, minus all the hair that had been shaved off when he joined the Army, so I didn't know what to think. I shrugged and decided it was okay if he was lying to me. He was cute, and it didn't matter to me if he was telling me a story just to sleep with me. He was younger than me, and I didn't think it was going to be a permanent relationship, anyway.

That first night, we just talked and fell asleep, cuddling. When we got up the next morning, Kyle told me he had never just slept in a bed with a woman without having sex before. He looked all bashful about it. By the quaver in his voice, I knew he was secretly a romantic. He was sweet and funny, very creative, and always composing song lyrics in our typing class that he gave to me. I was sad when we went our separate ways when the Army assigned us to different military bases, but I hadn't expected anything else.

The first Army post I was assigned to after I finished my training was Fort Stewart, Georgia. I worked at Fort Stewart for a year, then the Army moved me to Heidelberg, West Germany, to work at Campbell Barracks. During the time I was stationed there, Germany was still divided into two countries, West Germany and East Germany, separated by the Berlin Wall. Germany reunited as a country on October 3, 1990, eleven months after the fall of the Berlin Wall and a full three years after I left.

One night, after arriving in Heidelberg, I was walking through the snow with the damp cold penetrating my military uniform and combat boots. Having grown up in warm, sunny Hawaii, I really hated it when my feet got cold! I still didn't have a car because I sent money home each month to help my mother feed my children.

I missed my daughters like crazy. I had only seen them once in three years because you either send money home or you buy a plane ticket to go home to see your kids. You can't do both. The hard part was knowing my kids would suffer and do without–without money or without me—no matter what choice I made. My mom paid for me to fly home once. I worried about what sacrifices she had made to buy my plane ticket, as Hawaii was on the other side of the world.

One of the benefits of being in the Army was that my children had access to free medical care because they were my dependents. My mom could take my kids to the military hospitals on the island to see the pediatrician, have checkups, shots, etc. I was providing for my children as best I could. Dad moved out of Mom's house to live with his girlfriend full-time. I was more than relieved. I could take a breather.

Walking home through the snow in Heidelberg, so far from Hawaii, I promised myself,

"Next year, I'm not going to be cold."

I had no idea that next year, I would be colder than I'd ever been in my life.

CHAPTER 5:

On a White Horse

"A woman has got to love a bad man once or twice in her life, to be thankful for a good one."
—Marjorie Kinnan Rawlings

My next love interest rode in on his white horse like the hero in every movie I'd ever seen. A protocol officer with the rank of Major, Josh was about 5' 9" to my almost 5 '3' and was trim, athletic, and slightly muscular with dark brown hair and blue eyes. His job as a US Army protocol officer in West Germany was to escort VIPs and dignitaries. For example, he escorted Caspar Weinberger, Secretary of Defense under President Ronald Reagan, from the Frankfurt Ap Main airport in Frankfurt, West Germany, to Campbell Barracks to meet with General Glen Otis, who, at the time, was the CINCUSAR (Commander in Chief United States Army Europe).

I met Josh at the Keyes building, where General Otis had his headquarters. It was a secure building, with military police at checkpoints. Anyone who worked there had to have a high-level security clearance. I had a secret clearance because, as a secretary, I typed up itineraries showing the schedules of where VIPs would be traveling at certain times or days. This information was classified. If our country's enemies had this information, assassination attempts could be planned. At first, it was exciting, and I felt important with my security clearance, but it soon got old. There were just too many times when we were on high alert.

There were several instances when everyone who worked in my building had to evacuate because of bomb threats from terrorist cells. I learned that these terrorist groups were usually the second generation of the Baader-Meinhof Gang (also known as the Red Army Faction) and another group called the Red Brigade from Italy. At least, this was what the rumors portrayed at the time. The real story was above my pay grade.

From various briefings that I tried not to fall asleep during, I was informed that the Baader-Meinhof Gang was a West German communist terrorist group. They were not only unhappy with the capitalist German government, but they were also upset about the presence of U.S. armed forces in Germany. The other threat, The Red Brigade, was a break-off group from the communist party in Italy that was responsible for the assassinations of some political figures in Italy.

Bomb-sniffing dogs were brought in each time to search the building and grounds. *Again! Can you all just leave me alone*? I would think impatiently. *I've got work to do! I'm trying to earn a living here. I've got kids to feed.*

That's right, Jade, another voice would sound in my head. *The terrorists want to blow up the building just to screw up your work day!*

My life became a slog. I worked during the day, took college classes at night at the post-education center, and walked home to my barracks in the dark. Rinse and repeat.

I didn't have friends at Heidelberg, only social acquaintances. Isolated, I didn't feel I could depend on anyone else. People came and went, just like Dave and Kyle. Still young and naive but bitter beyond my years, I'd learned quickly that other people always let you down. *Just wait for it; it will happen.*

I shared a barracks room with another female soldier, Joyce, whom I barely had any contact with. She usually wasn't in the room when I was, or I was sleeping when she came in. Joyce was an E-3, PFC (Private First Class) in her early thirties, from the South. Her thick, straight brown hair was cut blunt at her shoulders with bangs, though she usually wore it up in a classy French twist when in uniform. Joyce had glasses, brown eyes, and a superior attitude toward others. She was divorced, like me, with kids back in the States, like me. You would have thought having so much in common would have made us besties. Not even close.

I was dressed in civvies when I first met her. She was chatty with me at first, until, "Oh, by the way, what rank are you?" she asked.

"I'm an E-4, Specialist Four."

Full stop. No more chattiness. The world had been put on pause. You could hear crickets.

Joyce suddenly found someplace she had to be.

Weird. It's not like I was going to give her any orders. Why some people think it's crucial to be the biggest tadpole in a tiny puddle, I don't know.

Just when I thought my slog of a life was all I would encounter in Germany, I met a handsome Army officer who was very suave and polished in his demeanor. Although he was primarily based in Frankfurt, I found out he came to Heidelberg several times a week to report to and receive orders from our commanding officer, Colonel Morton. When I first saw the Major, I thought, *ooh! Mr. Fancy, looking nice in his pants-y! Nice butt.* I almost bit my lip off, looking at him. Over the following weeks, I frequently caught him looking at me, too, checking me out. *Hmmm, this could be interesting.*

One day, I walked over to him and asked, "Can I get anything for you, Sir?" I stared right into his bright blue eyes.

"Ah, is my scheduling completed? Everything confirmed?"

"Yes, it is, Sir. I did it myself."

Glancing at the nametag on my uniform, he said, "Ah, good job, Specialist Parker."

"That's Specialist *Jade* Parker, Sir. So, tell me, Major Evans, what's your first name, if you don't mind me asking?"

"It's Josh. Nice to meet you, Jade."

While we made small talk, I gauged his reaction to me while keeping a poker face. I hadn't worked in a Korean bar for nothing! *He's trying to be cool, but he's interested. Yesss!*

"My pleasure, Sir, anytime. Just let me know if you need anything. Anything at all." *Wow, someone hold me back! I could get into trouble for this. Could you be any more obvious, Jade?*

This dance of back-and-forth flirting continued whenever Josh showed up at my office to meet with Colonel Morton. I was fascinated by him, and it was growing more apparent that he felt the same way about me. Still, he was more cautious than I was. I understood why he was being careful, but after several weeks, I started getting impatient. Ruefully, I thought, *why can't humans be like penguins during mating season, where the male penguin gives a pebble to the female penguin to secure her affection? Easy-peasy, right? Just hurry up and give me a dang pebble, Josh! We both know this relationship is going to happen!*

I learned that Josh grew up in Pennsylvania to a devout Catholic family, but later converted to the Church of Jesus Christ of Latter-day Saints in his twenties. His family wasn't happy about that at all. I was intrigued as I hadn't dated anyone with a strong spiritual or religious life. Now in his mid-thirties, I discovered that Josh had no children and had never been married. My impression of him was that he was a successful Army officer who had focused wholeheartedly on his career and seemed to live his life by the highest ethics.

That became even more apparent when he led us in to privately see our commanding officer, Colonel Morton, before our first official date. Fraternization between officers and enlisted personnel was frowned upon in the Army and could get us into trouble. The Colonel was sitting behind his desk and motioned for us to sit in the two chairs in front of him.

"So, what's this all about?" he asked, raising his eyebrows.

"Sir, Specialist Parker and I would like your permission to see each other, off duty."

A big smile spread across Colonel Morton's face, and I knew that we were lucky. This man was a romantic! A tall, slim, rugged man in his early fifties with silver-streaked hair and a granite face, the Colonel might have been as tough as a Sherman tank, but he was a softie inside.

"You have my permission, Major and Specialist, and good luck to the two of you," he said, still smiling, as he repositioned one of his pencils that had somehow stepped out of perfect formation on his desktop. We all shook hands and went back to work.

After work, Joyce happened to be in our barracks room when Josh came over to pick me up for our date. I had warned her a first date was coming, and she simply shrugged and blew me off, as she often did.

Knock, knock, knock, sounded the door, and when Joyce went over to open it, her mouth dropped open in surprise. She turned and gaped at me. *I can't believe you're dating an officer,* her face seemed to say.

Funny, but her behavior toward me seemed to change after that. Magically, she seemed to have gotten over her resentment of me outranking her and spent more time chatting with me. I could only guess that I was somehow worth her time to know now that I was dating a Major. Her behavior puzzled me. I was still the same person I was before dating Josh. It reminded me of when my mother wished she had bought my friend a better present due to her father's officer status. I didn't play those games in my mind. While I respected authority, I knew no one was better than another because of rank.

On our dates, I got to know both Josh and German culture better. He showed me a whole new world because he spoke fluent German. Everywhere we went, he translated for me. We ate at local restaurants, dining on chicken cordon bleu and sauerbraten. As I got to know him, I thought, *Josh is a good man! He goes to church every Sunday. He doesn't smoke, he doesn't drink, he doesn't cuss.* That was so new for me. *Besides, he's responsible, competent, and gets along with others. People like him. He's successful and works hard.*

I started attending church services at the Church of Jesus Christ of Latter-day Saints with Josh. I had heard of the Mormon church because of the Polynesian Cultural Center in Hawaii, but I had never met any Mormons—except for one ignorant jerk who asked me to be his second wife when I was just a sixteen-year-old. My encounter with him had left me with negative feelings about Mormons because there was no way I was going to be with that *moke* (a Hawaiian word for a local yokel, meaning an island-born man who is incredibly uneducated and uncultured and possibly in-bred). I didn't even know if he was, in fact, a Mormon or was telling me a story, trying to seduce me. Ugh!

With a little trepidation, I stepped into the clean halls of the church. There, I found the church members to be friendly and *normal*, not weird at all. I loved that it was a very welcoming, family atmosphere. I had rarely in my life, if ever, experienced such a strong sense of community, and to my astonishment, I quickly felt at ease there.

Josh was happy when I attended church services with him. We grew closer and closer. I knew we were meant to be together. I felt like I had won the lottery with this man, Major or not, and was giddy with happiness.

CHAPTER 6

Bliss to Eggshells

"A woman's heart should be so hidden in God that a man has to seek Him just to find her."
—Max Lucado

J osh and I continued to date and spend time with each other whenever we could. Due to our schedules, that was about twice a week. I was astonished that we became an exclusive couple from the beginning. While I was still working and living in Heidelberg, Josh was living in Frankfurt and traveling from Frankfurt to Heidelberg for work. Fortunately, we saw each other often.

As we grew closer, we discussed our future together. Cuddling on the couch and watching a video at Josh's apartment one night, he said, "I can't wait to have children one day. How do you feel about having more children in addition to Danni and Shayna?" I was quiet, dreading how to answer.

"Josh, I don't know how to tell you this, but here goes … I can't have any more children." I gulped, the tears rising to overflow down my cheeks, my throat tight. "When I was a single mother in Hawaii, I had my tubes tied. Josh, I couldn't even feed my own kids! I made the decision that I would never bring any more children into the world that I couldn't care for. It was the responsible thing to do."

Josh was quiet, and I waited for him to speak, hopeful but not expecting anything from him. After a while, he smiled.

"Well, you have two children, Jade. I could still be a father if things work out between us."

I gasped and sobbed with relief and joy. Although I didn't fully believe his words, I nodded my head, tears running down my face as he held me tightly in his arms. I cried for a long time, my painful memories washing over me.

As spring turned into summer and the trees became lush with green leaves, Josh asked me to marry him. This surprised me, although I had learned by now that he was a man who could be counted on to do what he said he would do. I enjoyed being with him immensely, but we'd only been dating for several months. *Is it too soon?*

Still, our commitment to each other was probably sped up significantly by the fact that my mother had grown ill. One day, I got a phone call from her saying she could no longer care for my two daughters.

Immediately, I applied for a compassionate discharge from the Army because I had to take over the care of my children. Mom had to rest so she could get well, which distressed and worried me. I'd been concerned about my mom's feelings about my dad moving out of their house. *You would think she would have thrown a party!* But instead, Mom's health went downhill. It was now evident to all extended family and neighbors that their marriage had failed, which was horribly shameful for my mom. Still, I had certainly been relieved and celebrated him not being around my daughters.

Rushed or not, I happily accepted Josh's marriage proposal, feeling loved for the first time in years. I had never believed men like him existed outside of the movies or romance novels! Certainly not any man I had met in my life. I was amazed and dumbfounded that he was willing to be a father to two children he had never met.

Thank you, God! I am so grateful that Josh is in my life. He's my hero.

My future life with Josh looked to be happy and serene. He had swept me completely off my feet. Stateside, I was discharged from the Army at Fort

Dix, New Jersey, and the two of us drove to Pennsylvania to meet his family. We were getting married there in about two weeks. I was beyond excited.

Then, I met Josh's parents.

The whole family, including Josh's brother and sister and their spouses, were sitting in the living room of Josh's parents' house, eating dinner and talking about everything and anything. We were having a good time, light-heartedly getting to know one another, laughing and having fun. As he talked to me, I thought Josh's dad was charming. He exuded charisma and bonhomie. I felt he was paying special attention to me, trying to draw me out, and welcoming me into the family, which made me happy. But when Josh's mom tried to join in with the fun conversation and dared to voice an opinion, Josh's dad irritably interrupted her.

"Shut up," he sneered contemptuously at her. "You're making a fool of yourself!"

Full stop. My mouth gaped open, and I was stunned by the viciousness in his voice! Suddenly, I didn't know what to do or how to feel. *What the hell?* I had the urge to slap him for her, even as she remained silent. Even more bizarre was how everyone in Josh's family acted as if nothing was wrong. His brother and sister and their spouses said nothing. Josh said nothing. His dad then turned back to me with a toothy smile, full of solicitude.

"So, how did you like being in the Army, Jade?"

"F-F-Fine," I stuttered, embarrassed at what I had witnessed, my eyes wide and shocked, my body rigid. I stared down at the plate of food in my lap, my fork gripped in my clenched fist, not feeling hungry anymore.

Josh's father continued talking to me, calmly and pleasantly, telling me of his own days in the military. I didn't hear most of what he said; I was just trying to recover my wits. I glanced up pointedly at Josh, making eye contact, bewildered, raising my eyebrows questioningly, but he just smiled back at me nonchalantly. Apparently, his father's behavior was nothing new.

As my fiancé and I quickly prepared for our upcoming wedding, I realized that the way Josh's dad treated his wife was normalized in their family. He criticized his wife endlessly, scoffing at her with vehement disdain and disgust. He was kind to me and others, but in a microsecond, he cut her to the bone with such thorough nastiness it took my breath away. Ugh! The tone of his voice when he talked to her hurt me the most.

Over the next two weeks, I watched Josh's mom run around, trying desperately to please her husband. No matter what he said to her, she never answered him back. Instead, she wore a tight, fixed, long-suffering smile on her face. I couldn't help but wonder, *was this a Catholic thing?*

Nevertheless, I was lovestruck with Josh. I took a breath and reminded myself that he didn't treat me like his dad treated his mom. So, just like the rest of Josh's family, I said nothing about his dad's behavior. I closed my eyes and ears like a coward to what was going on right in front of me because I didn't want to rock the boat so early with the family.

After our happy wedding and short but wonderful honeymoon, Josh and I flew back to West Germany for him to continue his military career and for me to be a housewife and full-time mother. Mom was planning to fly in from Hawaii with my daughters, and all three of them would meet Josh for the first time. I was out of my mind with happiness at the excitement of getting my children back. I hadn't seen them in two years. I was so thankful to be a mom and a housewife again. *Fingers crossed! It will be perfect this time, finally.*

My young daughters loved Josh as soon as they met him. When they got off the plane in Germany with my mom, six-year-old Danni looked up at Josh with big eyes and asked, "Are you going to be our daddy now?"

Shayna, two years younger, stood by her sister, quietly watching Josh, too. They had no memories of their own father.

"Yes, I am," said Josh, smiling warmly. In no time, they were holding hands and quickly trusted him. I watched it all.

I could also see why my mom needed some rest. Her eyes were hollow and sunken, her skin sallow and a color that just "wasn't right." She had lost weight, and her energy was incredibly low. She was going to stay with us for two to three weeks, and I was glad that she could rest and we could get caught up with events that were going on in both of our lives. Maybe I could feed her better so she could regain some of the vitality she used to have in my childhood.

I realized it takes a big, big man to take on the care of two children who are not his. We were a family of four now, and as grateful as I was, I knew it would take time for all of us to adjust. We all attended meetings at the Church of Jesus Christ of Latter-day Saints and were baptized into the church. Josh and I were sealed to each other in a ceremony for time and all eternity in the Frankfurt temple, and then my two sweet daughters were sealed to us.

After my baptism, I was given my patriarchal blessing by a higher priest in the church. A patriarchal blessing is an individualized session of life guidance where you are told about your future and the promised blessings that will come to you if you are faithful to God. It is as if Heavenly Father is talking to you by the Holy Spirit through the patriarch. I had never met the priest who gave me the blessing, and he didn't know me from Eve.

Surprisingly, among the many things he told me, he said I would bring more children into this world. Confused, I wondered if he could be mistaken because my tubes were tied, and I was physically unable to have any more children. I thought he was probably a little off in his telling me about what he saw for me in my future, but then I remembered that prophets could see around corners, so I put it in the back of my mind to wait and see. Puzzled, I wondered, *did I even want more children?*

I was delighted as Josh jumped headfirst into fatherhood, thoroughly enjoying having a family. He was a diligent and careful father. Sure, there was a learning curve for him, and he wasn't perfect, but he didn't have to be. I watched in awe as he took every opportunity to promote social and leadership skills in our girls as he took them to sports games, especially women's sports, from a young age. I watched them grow in confidence and strength. He would be the reason my two daughters would become the strong, independent, and fierce women of their futures, off conquering the world. It was no small task, and I was incredibly grateful for him in that respect, every day.

Unfortunately, although an excellent father, Josh turned out to be not such a great husband. It wasn't long after the girls got settled before the relationship between Josh and I started to deteriorate. At first, I didn't notice Josh's behavior changing. There were many, many good days… happy days with my children and Josh. I chalked up any unpleasantness to us being newly married and needing time to get used to each other's ways and truly settle in.

But one day, Josh came home from work and completely dogged me out for something I didn't do—something I didn't even know I was supposed to do! His complaints were vague, but his face was red, and he was seething with anger. In truth, he was stewing in it. Then, he complained about my not cleaning something and stormed off.

Shocked, I tried to get him to tell me what I didn't do so that I could do it, but he refused to talk to me. He just went into another room, angry as all get out, shut the door, and refused to give me a single explanation.

For the rest of the day, I was walking on eggshells. I would get used to these bewildering displays of malice and discontent, not quickly, but gradually. I was like a frog in a pot of water where the heat is turned up incrementally until the water boils, and the frog is dead. I hated being in hot water with him, but I could never get out. Only later did I realize it was the same place where Josh's dad wanted Josh's mom to be—helpless in the boiling water of his wrath and derision.

My husband began withholding and withdrawing from me when he was angry, which was happening more and more often. Then, one night, Josh stopped having sex with me. Crushed and bewildered, I lay on my side of the bed, sure this would pass. Eventually, I went to him and begged for affection. I couldn't understand how he could act like the perfect husband when we went to church or a social event, but he was a very different person at home where no one could see him. When he was angry, he wouldn't talk to me, and he wouldn't touch me. He would just give me scathing looks full of scorn and contempt. It hurt badly that he didn't like holding my hand or cuddling me in his arms any longer. He showed much more affection to our cats, Boodles and Wonky-Pooh, than he ever showed me. It soon became a frigid marriage, like the flakes of snow tumbling to the ground in Frankfurt. I spent hours in the night just staring out the frozen windowpanes.

After about a year, when Josh was reassigned from West Germany to Fort McPherson, right outside Atlanta, Georgia, I prayed for a new beginning. We moved our family into a big, beautiful house that I never would have imagined, a year-and-a-half earlier, I would ever live in. Instead of a fresh new start, the relationship between Josh and I worsened.

My mother adored Josh, and now that she'd been able to rest and recuperate, she visited us often. However long she stayed with us, she bent over backward, catering to him the whole time she was with us. She wouldn't let anyone eat until Josh came home, and then she would quickly stir-fry dinner for us so that she could serve him a fresh, hot meal.

Josh would grouse at me right in front of my mom, "Why don't you take care of me like your mom does?" I just shook my head. I *did* do those things. I cared for the house, cared for the girls, and took them to all the sports and leadership functions he signed them up for whenever he had to be working.

As much as I wanted to, I couldn't tell Mom how unhappy I was. Compared to the life she had lived with my dad, I had won the jackpot! She had no idea what our relationship was really like. I was either boiling or freezing to death, and I was always starving for affection in our marriage. Josh and I were still going without any sex for significant periods of time.

However, there were a few times when my mother saw Josh's anger explode. He held his cool more easily in front of her. One time, when she was visiting us, she made hot rice and stir-fried beef with vegetables. She worked hard to thinly slice the carrots, string beans, celery, onions, bamboo shoots, and ginger so she could stir fry them in minutes. The night before, Josh had told my mother that he was having problems with his blood pressure and couldn't eat salt. Of course, I didn't mention that his constantly simmering rage didn't help his high blood pressure, but it was obvious to me.

That next evening, my mother left all the salt and soy sauce out of the dinner. She wanted to make it perfect for her son-in-law. When she served him his dinner, he took a bite, and his face twisted up. He chewed, swallowed, and then abruptly rose from the table.

"This food is awful!" he stated furiously, throwing his napkin down. He stalked out of the room, down the hall into his office, and slammed the door with a decided *thud.* My mother just looked at me and threw the rest of the food in the trash.

"Do you think he wants me to make him something else?" she asked me.

Tiptoeing now on the eggshells strewn about my nice, clean house, I said, "No, Mom, don't cook him anything more." I knew he would stay in his office for a long while, the door shut.

Josh had trouble letting go of stress and would often look calmer after he got home and took out the stresses of his day on me. It became a daily ritual: he would follow me around the house, criticizing how I dressed, what I ate, even how I chewed my food, *ad infinitum.* He even complained about the way I breathed. He watched me like a hawk and jumped on me the moment I did anything that he could criticize me about. He talked to me with a horrific tone of contempt in his voice—of course, only when we were alone so no one else would witness it. After he had reduced me to tears, he seemed to calm down and looked more relaxed, and would walk away, satisfied.

As the months passed, the same toxic patterns in our marriage kept going around and around like a needle on a broken record. I cared for our children and the house and attended church on Sundays with my family. I began attending our church's temple for solace at least once a week during the day while my kids were at school. I loved going to the temple. It was a sacred place, and I wished I could stay there all the time because I felt God's presence there and longed to be close to Him. I prayed unceasingly to my Father, talking to him about how I felt and how unhappy I was in my marriage. I wondered, *am I that unworthy of love that my own husband doesn't love me? Heavenly Father, whatever happened to the admonition to the men of the Church to love their wives "with love unfeigned"?*

All I wanted was to be a good Mormon wife. I tried everything to make Josh happy. He sometimes seemed happy for a moment, but never stayed happy for long. If he came home angry from work, it was my fault. No kidding. If the weather outside was bad, he groused at me as if it was my fault! There was no reasoning with him. I stopped fighting back after a while. Slowly, I was being ground down to nothing. Erased. My opinions were stupid. My feelings were unimportant. As fall turned into winter, I became depressed.

"Josh, I'm really unhappy," I admitted honestly. "Can we talk about it?"

"Why don't you go see a doctor and take a pill for it?" he said, irritated. Then, he walked away.

I felt like a failure. My self-esteem had become shredded. Josh didn't want to have to deal with my weaknesses or accept any responsibility for his part in my unhappiness. He didn't want to be bothered with any of my needs. If *he* needed something, however, I was to snap to it. That was wearing on me, as well. I started fighting back again, but knowing my words were useless against his scathing arguments, I resorted to throwing things. I didn't realize he had me again, right where he wanted me.

I became somewhat hopeful when Josh agreed to go to marriage counseling with me at a local counseling center. As we sat there in the therapist's office, he took great pride in telling her that he had never been physically violent with me. Instead, I admitted that I threw things at him: cups, books, bowls, anything close by that I could grab in my anger. I admitted I had gotten to the point where I wanted to wipe that contemptuous look of superiority off his face when he would follow me around the house, picking, prodding, and berating me until I lost my temper.

I didn't like to be ugly, so I could never match him in words. I tried to defend myself by throwing something at him to make him leave me alone. He would just stand there with a look of cold disdain while I screamed, hurt and confused as to why I could never do anything to make him happy. Once, I even grabbed and threw my cat, Boodles, at Josh. Boodles went airborne and landed on Josh with twenty claws extended. Got him good.

Fortunately, Boodles wasn't hurt. Josh's rage and contempt was just for me, and I never put another creature in danger, again.

We didn't last long in marriage counseling—maybe five sessions. Nothing changed. I finally asked for help from the bishop of our ward—our church leader. It was embarrassing for me, but I was desperate. I asked him to talk to my husband because of his mentally and emotionally abusive behavior. He counseled us separately, but still, my husband's behavior never changed.

I never knew what our bishop said to Josh, but as I was getting up to leave his office after a particularly shattering altercation with Josh's mean fury, the only advice the bishop had to give me was, "You need to be patient, Jade."

Too little, too late, I thought. That was the last time I asked for help with my marriage problems from any of the priesthood of the church. Going to the bishop had been my last resort. That night, as I lay in bed, stuck like glue to my own side of the mattress, I came to a decision.

Josh is not going to change, I thought. *He's hardwired the way he is. So, what am I to wait and be patient for? Wait and be patient for a miracle from God? Wait and be patient, and put up with Josh's abusive treatment of me till my youth is gone, the years passing as he grinds me into the dust, my agency erased until I finally die?* I felt like an old geisha in a Korean bar, wearing out past her prime with nothing left. *What would that accomplish, except killing everything that makes me unique as a soul?*

Of course, Josh was angry with me that I complained about him to our bishop, and now I had a feeling that if he could, he would try to find a reason to show the bishop that I was the problem, not him.

I was angry and disillusioned, too. I felt I had been promised a happy marriage when I converted to the Church and was baptized. *What happened?*

I prayed, and prayed, and prayed, my face wet and swollen from crying. *Where are you, Heavenly Father? Why am I in this agonizing situation?* I knew the relationship I had with Josh was not the relationship my Heavenly Father wanted for me, His beloved daughter. *This is not my destiny. It can't be.*

I felt trapped and kept praying. *What should I do?* I had gotten the care of my children back a couple of years earlier from my mother. I couldn't uproot my children again, especially now that Danni was eight and Shayna was six. I thought, *they love Josh! He's the only father they've ever known. How can I take that away from them?*

CHAPTER 7:

The Miracle

"Have you ever been in love? Horrible, isn't it? It makes you so vulnerable. It opens your chest, and it opens up your heart and it means that someone can get inside you and mess you up."
—Neil Gaiman

I walked through my gorgeous house that morning, gathering pills as I went. It was a big, spacious house with a lot more bedrooms than we had people—a McMansion. Since moving in not quite two years ago, I had tried my best, but I never did figure out what to do with some of the rooms. Their higher purposes unrealized, they became dusty, gathering junk and empty boxes. Walking through the modern white and chrome kitchen, I checked the cabinet where we kept medicines.

Thinking back on my life before I married Josh, I never dreamed I would ever live in a house like this, but here I was. As I perched on the closed toilet seat in our huge master bathroom, I poured my heart out to my Heavenly Father. Josh was at work, and my children were at school. I was alone.

"Father, I can't do it anymore," I cried aloud. "Please, I want to go home. It's been more than I've been able to deal with. I'm sorry, but I just want to go home."

Scooping up half of the pills I had gathered from around the house, I swallowed them down with a plastic toothbrush cup filled with water. Wiping the tears from my face, I looked at the other half of the pills piled on the granite countertop. It was almost over. As a mother, I was a failure. As for being a good wife to my husband, I had failed at that, too. But more deeply than either of those, I felt my failure as a daughter of God.

Why would I want to live in my head anymore? My own derisive thoughts about myself often replaced Josh's voice in my mind. I couldn't take the self-loathing, the hate. Because it was too painful to be who I was, I just wanted to be erased, to have an end to my suffering.

Many times, I had prayed to my Heavenly Father, but I had received no answers. Exhausted from trying to meet my husband's unrealistic expectations, my harsh memories whirled and exploded in my head. Josh treated me as if I was worthless, so maybe I didn't even have the right to be alive. Maybe I should have been aborted before I was born.

After all, I had been put up for adoption before I was born. Why didn't my birth mother have an abortion? I knew she had been a teenager who had gotten pregnant by a married man when she was just seventeen years old. I'd accessed the court records by calling the family court in Honolulu. The judge who had handled my adoption years before called my adoptive parents to read them parts of my file and the information that was available about my biological parents so they could relay that information to me. I found out that my biological mother had had a tragic life of foster care and being unwanted.

My birth mother had met a man while she was pregnant with me. He wanted to marry her, but he didn't want the baby she was carrying inside her because the baby wasn't his. She had to choose between keeping the child she was carrying and the man who could offer her a better life. It was apparently just one of the many hard decisions she made in her life. She chose him.

After I had processed the information I had about my birth, I felt confused. I felt as if I had been thrown away like a piece of trash, a piece of garbage. This feeling squatted at the core of my being for most of my life.

I never felt worthy or good enough. As much as I wanted to, I couldn't completely comprehend that I was a beloved daughter of God and that a beloved daughter of God is never trash but is infinitely precious to our Heavenly Father and Jesus Christ.

I never found God or Jesus Christ while growing up in my family or in the Congregational church I was sent to on Sundays. I didn't even find Him in the services I attended with the Jehovah's Witnesses when I was a young teen. Sobbing and praying now in the bathroom of our McMansion, I was trying to get up the courage to take the last handful of pills.

Suddenly, my body was jerked upright by an electric feeling, like a bolt of lightning running up and down from my head to my toes. It was too soon for any of the pills to have taken effect. *What is this?*

An abrupt, pulling-like pressure made me feel as if the top of my head had been opened, and someone was pouring something like water into the top of my head. The feelings of swirling water merged with words that were put into my thoughts, and although I didn't hear with my ears, I knew the words that were spoken to me.

"No matter what happens to you in this life, you're going to be okay."

Then, I was engulfed by a powerful, very certain feeling of love that surrounded and covered me like a blanket, thick and protective.

I gasped and kept gasping. Never had I experienced anything like this in my life! Stunned by the overwhelming feelings of love and peace surrounding me, I was finally able to cry and pray aloud to my Heavenly Father, thanking Him. I believed the assurance I had received. I knew I was going to be alright.

Exhausted by the experience and my emotions, I sat there for a long, long moment. Then, decidedly, I rose and flushed the rest of the pills down the toilet, and despite the afternoon hour, I went to bed.

Later that evening, Josh came home to find me in bed. I was so grateful for the miracle that had saved my life, but my body was still feeling very sick—nauseous and woozy, a consequence of the pills I had taken.

"I took a whole bunch of pills," I admitted, slurring.

Josh didn't say anything. He just looked at me with his usual derision and scorn, then got in on his side of the bed and went to sleep.

I was sick for about a week after I tried to kill myself. When I looked in the mirror, my face was so pale. Realizing I must have trashed my liver with all the pills I took, I became certain I would have wound up in the hospital—or dead—if I had finished taking all of the pills.

It truly was a miracle that I survived, and I knew Who was behind it. I was grateful, but I didn't know what to do with what I'd been told. *"No matter what happens to you in this life, you're going to be okay."* As comforting as it felt in the moment, what the hell did that even mean for the rest of my life?

As soon as I recovered, I moved into a spare bedroom in my house. I didn't want to sleep in the same bedroom, and certainly not in the same bed with Josh anymore. I stopped caring that we weren't having sex. I was completely fed up with my husband. I stopped blaming myself. *Hmmm, I wonder how Josh will like having to tiptoe on eggshells around me!*

Although I had experienced a miracle, it didn't change the troubles in my marriage to Josh. Nothing had changed there. I could have used a miracle from God to change Josh, but I guess that was not God's plan. And since Josh was always right and I was always wrong, why would Josh change what wasn't broken?

The miracle I experienced from my Heavenly Father gave me the courage to go on with my life. I finally felt loved despite everything that was wrong with me and all the things I had done wrong. I started to fight *for* my life instead of giving up and giving in to Josh's emotional blackmail. Now, I knew my Heavenly Father valued and cherished me, even if Josh didn't. I decided that since Josh wouldn't change, I had to change. I started to work on myself. *What do I want?*

Despite the miracle and the love I felt from my Heavenly Father, I stopped going to church. I couldn't stand Josh's fake, self-righteous attitude. Josh's cardboard cut-out of his perfect family made me sick to my stomach, and I wanted no part of it.

I started going out with various girlfriends from my college courses, drinking at bars. No more crying over Josh's treatment of me. Instead, I decided to completely stop caring what he thought. My new viewpoint was driven by a rage that wouldn't quit. Josh so badly needed to feel superior to me that he didn't care if his denigration of me brought me so low that I considered suicide. It was his constant drip, drip, drip, like a leaky faucet, that I was stupid, worthless, and nothing, that had led me to despair.

Furious over how I had almost killed myself over Josh's toxic, emotional blackmail, I vowed to never again let someone else determine my worth.

I started taking some small steps to figure out what I wanted out of life and how to get it. My top priority was leaving Josh. I had started my college degree while I was in the Army, and I needed to finish it. I went to work with a new plan to study hard and finish my pre-nursing, making sure to enclose my pre-nursing credits into both an associate in liberal arts degree and a bachelor of arts degree in administration. I didn't know when I would be able to go to nursing school, but I knew that if the credits were not enclosed in a degree, I might lose them if too much time passed before I started nursing school. I wasn't taking any chances. There was too much at stake.

Determined to move on with my life, I decided to enlist in the Army Reserves as a means of finding some independence from Josh and my unhappy marriage.

Unfortunately, I enlisted in the Army Reserves just in time for the start of the Gulf War, when Iraq invaded Kuwait. George H. W. Bush was President of the United States of America. Many of the soldiers in my Reserve unit were caught by surprise, including me. No one had expected to go to war.

I was assigned to an airborne Military Intelligence unit, which was part of a rapid response battalion sent to the Gulf. Military Intelligence (MI) personnel are trained as spies, interrogators, and to collect and analyze surveillance, in addition to other jobs. Because I was the company secretary, I would also attend training with the MI personnel, taking classes, for example, on how to conduct interrogations (not in a nice way). Weird, but interesting. I decided MI guys were crazy.

There was a list of people from my unit who were called up to go to the Gulf, but my name never came up. I guess they decided to keep me

Stateside to handle the paperwork at the home unit. I thanked God I did not have to leave my girls again.

I left the Army Reserves shortly after the Gulf War ended, right before I was due to be sent to Airborne school or "Jump School," which was probably a good thing. In Jump School, you learn how to jump out of an aircraft and land safely using a parachute. You're supposed to hit the ground running and move on to your site of combat operations.

I was told by other soldiers who had graduated that when you're in that plane, flying high in the sky, there are only *two* ways for a trainee to get off that plane: you either jump off the plane or the instructor will throw you off! Either way, you are getting off the plane. After my experience with Drill Sergeant Reece and Drill Sergeant Willis, I had no reason to doubt that what they were telling me was the truth.

When my time in the Army Reserves ended, I was incredibly relieved that I hadn't been sent to the Gulf for Operation Desert Shield and Operation Desert Storm under the leadership of *Stormin' Norman*, General Norman Schwarzkopf. Going to the Gulf War might have been the experience of a lifetime, but I might also have been exposed to Sarin gas when the chemical weapons facilities were bombed in Iraq. I'd had enough of being gassed in boot camp; I was happy to take a pass.

CHAPTER 8:

Good Intentions 101

"Macho does not prove mucho."
—Zsa Zsa Gabor

It takes a fool to make an enemy out of his own wife, I thought. And I was looking at one right now. I was in a crowded bar, music on the dance floor blaring. Hot and sweaty people dancing, drinking, loud voices, cigarette smoke fogging the air, people everywhere talking, laughing. It was bedlam—a normal night out at the clubs with Jennie.

A short, muscular man in a sweatshirt jacket confronted me as I sat at the bar drinking and chilling to the music.

"Where's Jennie?" he demanded.

My stomach made a quick dive to the floor because I was fairly certain where Jennie was. My friend, the EMT and fellow college student, was in the parking lot making out in a car with a guy she'd met here a little while ago. Her husband was now standing in front of me, looking for her.

Jennie was a sweet-faced, almost 5'9" blond with a killer bod and a fetish for short men. Her thing wasn't "little people," but still very short men about 5' to 5'5". Earlier that night, she had got up off the barstool next to me, saying, "See you in a little bit," and walked over to chat up a very cute guy about 5 '4'' tall on the other side of the bar. From the look on Jennie's face, I knew he was lunch meat. They walked out of the bar a few minutes later, and I was just relaxing and listening to the music when the jerk, her husband, showed up.

"Where's Jennie?" he repeated.

He must have got off early from his work shift, I thought, trying not to panic. *Oh crap, what am I going to do?*

"She's around here somewhere. Here, let me go look for her," I offered and darted off as fast as I could, with him trailing me through the thick crowds of people in his way.

I walked past the women's bathroom and saw a sign on the door, "Out of Order." I quickly pushed the door open on the off chance Jennie was in there. She wasn't, but someone was vomiting loudly behind the closed door of one of the stalls. Thinking quickly, I ripped the sign off the door, mashed it into a ball, and rolled it under the nearest table, just in time for Jennie's husband to catch up to me.

"She's had too much to drink, and she's barfing in the bathroom," I said. I swung open the bathroom door to the sounds of moaning and vomiting coming from one of the stalls.

"Is that Jennie in there?" he asked. "Jennie, are you okay?"

No answer from the stall except moaning. "You can't come in here; it's the women's bathroom," I said, blocking the door from him entering. "Why don't you go have a drink, and I'll look after her. She'll come out when she feels better."

He didn't like it but agreed and strode away to get a drink and wait at the bar. I snuck around the side of the bar and made a quick getaway outside to find Jennie.

Fortunately, I met her just in time, just as she was about to come back into the bar with her new boy toy. I pulled her to me under the cover of giving her a hug and whispered, "Your husband's here! Get rid of the toy and meet me at the bar. You've been drunk, throwing up in the bathroom— that's why we couldn't find you. Go!" I turned around, backtracked to the women's bathroom, and then casually joined Jennie's husband at the bar.

"Jennie's feeling much better. She's cleaning up, and she'll join us soon."

Jennie walked up to us a while later and quickly went home with her husband, complaining she'd had too much to drink. I didn't like to lie, but Jennie's husband beat her regularly for no reason at all. If he had found out what she'd been doing, I knew he would have killed her.

Jennie didn't start her marriage being unfaithful to her husband. Neither did I. Both of us had married for love. But Jennie's husband had turned out to be a violent man, and he beat her just because he wanted to. Because that's the kind of sick, tiny man he was. Josh didn't beat me, but he was cruel to me, mentally and emotionally, and used me to relieve his stress.

After I had stopped caring what he thought about me, I asked him, "Did you know, Josh? It takes a fool to make an enemy out of his own wife."

I didn't know why some men thought they could abuse a woman and expect her to just take it, not hate him, and not fight back! I had been faithful to Josh up until I tried to kill myself. But now, all bets were off! Josh's behavior toward me left me feeling unwanted and unloved, but if he didn't want me, someone else would. I don't know if Josh was ever unfaithful to me during our marriage. He was very secretive about certain parts of his life. All I knew was that he wasn't having sex with me.

When Jennie and I met while taking pre-nursing classes, we bonded immediately because we both had unhappy marriages. She was originally from Brooklyn, New York, and was working part-time as an EMT (Emergency Medical Technician) where we were living, in Georgia. She had two kids, just like me, and was studying to become a nurse so she could afford to leave her husband, like me.

I woke up one morning to find her sleeping in her car in my driveway because her husband had beaten her up the night before. She had somehow gotten away from him. He wouldn't beat her kids because she was the one he was so focused on manipulating, denigrating, and controlling. She was the scapegoat. I knew precisely what it was like to be the scapegoat in the family.

She called me another night, crying, "Jade, please come over right now," she begged. "Please, I need you," and she hung up.

I drove like a madwoman to her house, running red lights.

Oh, crap! I thought. *He beat her again, and she killed him! Where the hell am I going to hide the body?*

I made a list in my mind of options as to where to dispose of a body as I drove.

Bury it in the woods, throw it in a dumpster, burn it in a car (no, that won't work), put it down a manhole, brick it up in a wall, dump it in a river, oil drum in the bottom of a lake, acid in a bathtub, find a pig farm... The list went on and on. I was entirely too educated from watching *CSI* on television.

I finally got to her apartment, and thank God, she answered my knock. There was no blood splatter from a dead body on the floor—only the soul-crushing reality of a shattered woman before me. He had beat her up again, to his satisfaction. Then, he simply left for work.

Our lives could not go on like this. Not for Jennie... nor for me.

CHAPTER 9:

An Interesting Idea

"When she was good, She was very good, indeed. But when she was bad, she was horrid."
—Henry Wadsworth Longfellow

One day, Jennie and I were studying for our pre-nursing exams together when she said, "Jade, I'm going for a job interview at a strip club. Do you want to come with me and apply for a job, too?

Sounds like an interesting idea, I thought. "Sure, I need a job," I said aloud. We both needed to make some money so we could leave our husbands. It was one way out of my situation because there was no way I would go back to live with my mother in Hawaii again.

I thought long and hard about whether it was the right thing to do. No excuses. I knew it was *not* the moral thing to do, but I was so unhappy and desperate in my marriage that I was willing to consider any possible solutions to my situation.

Finally, I decided that working as a dancer in a strip club was a short-term means to an end. Get in, get my money, and get out. I needed financial independence and freedom from Josh. I needed to find a solution to get out on my own and provide a safe home for my children. The real, long-term solution was to get as much education as I could to launch a well-paid career, but it would also be helpful to have an emergency fund in case things went sideways in the meantime. I decided to do both education *and* exotic dancing to provide myself with options. Strategically, I thought, *know what your plan is and don't go in blind.*

Jennie and I showed up at the club and were interviewed. I was surprised when we were both hired. We started work the next night.

The rules were explained to us. No letting the customers touch us, no prostitution, and no walking into the club at the start of our shift looking anything other than gorgeous. Like at the Korean bar, we were told that we were selling every man his fantasy. Only here, we had to become his dream of the ideal woman, needing to look drop-dead gorgeous from the time we walked in the door to go backstage to when we left the club at the end of our shift. No sloppy clothes, no dirty hair. Full makeup and sexy, sexy, sexy outfits were mandatory.

I found out that looking beautiful was exhausting work. It's not easy looking over-the-top hot all the time, especially when you're sweating from dancing and your feet hurt from the stilettos you wear all shift. Hair gets tangled and limp, and makeup runs down your face with sweat if you don't keep touching it up. All the dancers kept makeup kits, curling irons, hairbrushes, combs, hair spray, and gel backstage at the tables with the lighted mirrors and chairs for them to sit and fix their makeup and hair between dancing sets. Backstage, we dressed into our skimpy outfits to take off when we danced on stage around a chrome stripper pole.

Jennie only worked a half-shift the first night and then quit. She spent some of the time hiding backstage because she recognized someone she worked with from the hospital, sitting at one of the tables out on the floor. Since Jennie was my ride to the club, I had to leave when she did, but I was back the next night to work a full shift, driving my own car.

Truth be told, I was a little ticked off that Jennie quit. I had never let go of a job that paid a living wage without it being pried from my dead, cold hands. Jennie was a little miffed that I didn't quit working as a stripper, even though it was her idea in the first place! She got over it when she saw that I was determined to work *the plan*: get in, get my money, and get out. Strictly business. For me, working as a stripper was not a job to make a career out of. I was tired of Josh using money to control and manipulate me.

So, I began working at the strip club in the evening, three to four times a week, after my kids were asleep and Josh was home. He didn't have a clue because I was also taking college classes in the afternoon and at night. I worked as a stripper on Friday and Saturday nights, for sure, because that's when it rained money. All the dancers also had to pull a shift on at least two other nights during the week to make sure that customers had a variety of girls dancing for them

I was backstage with the other dancers, getting ready to go on shift one late afternoon, when two guys showed up backstage to fix something electrical. The house mother, also known as the mama-san, was showing them what needed to be done, but they just stared at all the naked and half-naked girls running around, getting ready to go onstage or out on the floor. They took forever to fix whatever needed to be fixed, and when the mama-san shooed them away out the door, they walked backward, very slowly, staring at us with wide eyes and smiles on their faces. It didn't bother us; we were used to men staring.

I always showed up for my shift at the strip club dressed to the nines, my dark hair loose and wavy down to the middle of my back. All the valets would hurry to get to my car first to open the door for me so I could swing my high-heeled legs and micro-mini skirt out of the car to walk into the club. I just smiled enticingly at them and sashayed through the front doors of the club, with all the men's eyes on me as I did my catwalk through the tables to go backstage.

That's right, Josh! I thought. *Suck it! Who wants me now, Josh?*

Just as it was at the Korean bar, prostitution was frowned upon and grounds for getting fired, but there were private rooms where customers could get a lap dance, and the boss usually looked the other way if any extra favors were transacted. Not for me. Not with total strangers at the strip club.

Then, there was the house mama, a three hundred pound 'truck driver-type' lesbian, who sat backstage and kept an eye on the girls. She would massage a girl's neck, back, or even feet if they asked her or get them something to eat or drink. At the end of the night, all the dancers would tip out ten percent to the bar, the bouncers, and the house mama/mama-san.

I didn't do any prostitution at the strip club because I was making more money than I ever dreamed of. Why take a chance on getting murdered by a stranger or catching a venereal disease when, for a lot less risk, I could still make a lot of money—at least five times more money on a good night than I made at the Korean bar and probably ten times more than what I made in the Army.

Now, I had a little bit of freedom and control. I had my own money, instead of Josh controlling and deciding what I could spend money on. Josh would often get impatient when I was shopping, no matter what I was shopping for, and would yell or gripe at me until I quit shopping and said I was done. He was always reluctant to spend money on what I wanted, except when he deemed it a worthy purchase—his decision, not mine.

As for my job at the strip club, I chose to conform to the stated, official rules. My motto was: Look, but don't touch. There was no way I was going to lose this job.

There were temptations and distractions at work. On Friday and Saturday nights, vendors set up displays of expensive clothes, jewelry, makeup, and other accouterments in the dancers' dressing room. I noticed other dancers spending the money they had just made dancing on-stage, like water! They acted as if there was a river of money that would never end. A lot of them spent so much money that they were as broke when they left the club that night as when they got there to start their shift!

Another problem was that there were a lot of drugs at the club. I was offered drugs almost every day. Girls would get hooked and have to continue to work as dancers because they needed the money to support their growing addiction. As time went on, their drug habits inevitably worsened, their lives imploded, their beauty faded, and they became such a mess they could no longer work at the club. I would hear about them working at strip clubs that catered to less-select clientele until the girls wound up working on a street corner, their drug habit all they had left.

Men would get angry when I wouldn't take their drugs. I knew better. I had two beautiful children at home. My agenda was not their agenda, and I avoided it at all costs.

I was wary of pimps showing up at our club, looking to add a new girl to their stable. They'd love-bomb a girl if they sensed blood in the water. If she didn't watch out, she would wind up working for him. Not for me. I saw what happened when her money became his money.

Guys from local rock bands also frequented the club, looking for beautiful dancers for girlfriends. This, they believed, shored up their image. *Yeah, baby, I'm living the life with my guitar and my stripper girlfriend!* I didn't like them. I noticed they were big talkers and often leeches without a recording contract or any serious money. They wanted to live off their dancer's money like a pimp. That was a dead end, too.

No, thank you. I had already experienced that during my childhood, with my dad constantly begging my mom for the money she worked hard for. Unfortunately, I had to deal with all these guys in addition to the usual creeps, perverts, drug dealers, rapists, criminals, and psychopaths.

I told myself, *No buying clothes, jewelry, or drugs. No finding a boyfriend or a girlfriend at the club. Everything must be strictly business. Take the cash and run.*

Unconsciously, in case something bad happened, I wanted to be prepared, just like my mom was always ready. After expenses, I saved every bit of the money I earned.

Through opportunities that were offered to me while I was working as a stripper, I became involved in a Sugar Baby/Sugar Daddy relationship several times. I don't know why some people who have lived that lifestyle argue that it's not prostitution. In my opinion, it is. It certainly was for me. I was also a once-in-a-while escort/girlfriend for some select, wealthy men. All of them were married. I never had a lot of clients, just a handful. It was a transactional relationship, where you were clearly exchanging sex for money. I mean, isn't that the definition of prostitution?

This was also a trap and a waste of my time. I wasn't in the lifestyle for long. *Get in, get your money, and get out,* I reminded myself. Although

I have never walked a street corner doing tricks, I realized I was not any better than those who have walked the streets. It's the same thing, except the bed you lie in is covered in sheets with a higher thread count.

During my time as a piece of arm candy, I would go on "dates" with a man, and there was never any confusion between the two of us that I would sleep with him and that he would give me money for doing so. I was picky about who I dated, however. I had to be picky because I was working in an often-dangerous job, and I am a very paranoid person. Luckily, I was aware enough to dodge some very unpleasant situations, and I kept myself and my body safe.

One sugar baby relationship I had was with a married reverend, a minister in a Christian church. One evening, I met him at his church because he was taking me out to dinner, and we were going to spend some time together. We were in the empty chapel—no one was there but us—and he got a phone call.

When he got off the phone, he said, "Sorry, babes, I gotta go."

He stuck his hand in the collection plate, grabbed a fistful of cash, and handed it to me. He then took more bills out of his wallet and gave them to me, also.

"Here, go shopping. I'm sorry about tonight."

I pocketed the cash, went shopping, and then drove home with my purchases: some Godiva chocolates and a beautiful white straw hat with black feathers. Josh saw me walk in the door with my two shopping bags from the mall and carry them up to my bedroom. We were now sleeping in separate bedrooms.

"And how much money did you spend, Jade?" he yelled at me, his face red and angry.

"Oh, don't worry about it, Josh. It wasn't your money that I spent. Even though you don't want me, other men do," I declared snidely. I slammed the door on his shocked face and thought, *Payback is a mother, and I am a mother. How you likin' them eggshells, Josh?*

I felt I had been cheated of the happy, loving marriage I thought Josh and the Church had promised me. That blissful union was one of the blessings

I was told I would have when I converted to the Church and was baptized. But it never happened—at least not with Josh, despite my prayers.

I had been working as a stripper and sugar baby for several months. Josh knew something was up. One night, after dancing, I came home late, walking in the door barefoot, carrying my heels, and tip-toeing my aching feet upstairs to my bedroom. Josh was sleeping in the master bedroom down the hall. I undressed and fell on the bed, exhausted. My hair smelled of sweat, cigarette smoke, and whiskey that someone spilled on me.

Suddenly, the bedroom door opened, and Josh bolted into the room.

"Jade, what's going on?" he asked.

My husband sounded, for once in a long time, genuinely concerned. I even had a passing thought. *Maybe we can start a dialogue, maybe start over.* I was so tired of running.

"Josh, I've been working as a dancer, a stripper," I admitted bleakly, too exhausted to explain any further. I looked at his shocked face and thought, *Good, it's out. He knows. Maybe we can start over.*

Josh started taking his clothes off.

"No!" I yelled. "I am not having sex with you! How many years has it been? And you want me *now*? Get away from me!"

Josh didn't stop undressing or coming for me. I finally just let him use my body. I didn't enjoy the sex we had, and he didn't care that I didn't want it. When he left the room, I numbly turned over and went to sleep. No tears. They were all gone a long time ago.

However, when Josh woke up the next day, he called the bishop and had me excommunicated. I felt abused and betrayed. I knew the stripping was wrong. What I was doing went against all the principles of the gospel I had been taught, and I felt bad, but I was so miserable I didn't care.

What do I do now? I was no longer a member of my church, and things were very tense in the house. I had to think of my future. *Do I divorce Josh? What about my handsome Ned?*

In addition to my clients, I had started seeing Ned, free of charge. A tall, good-looking marine I had met while taking night classes, Ned had light brown hair buzzed short around his ears and nape in a "jarhead" haircut. I loved the smell of his skin, musky and sweaty. Ned had never been married and had no children. He knew I was working at the strip club and that I dated men who paid me for my time. We had started with a "one-time only" fling, but it had developed into something more.

"Have you thought about us being together, Jade?" Ned had casually asked me one night in bed.

It was quiet... *too quiet.* I was struggling to think, struggling for words. *What should I say?* He knew how I felt about him, but my obsession with him wasn't enough. You can't make a relationship out of sex.

"I like things the way they are, Ned. Let's not ruin it, okay?" I finally breathed.

Ned's face had a look of sad, resigned understanding. He wanted to take our relationship to the next level, but I refused to give him a chance to do so. There was a possibility that I could have found happiness with him, but I had to think of my children. Ned had no track record as a father. I couldn't help but think, *how would he treat my children?* As tempting as it was to contemplate, I checked myself. *Better the devil you know than the devil you don't.*

Because that's the one thing I knew about Josh—he enjoyed being a father. He was careful to make sure that the girls did their homework and that the management of the family was done properly. For that reason only, I put up with the abuse Josh meted out to me, determined to leave after my children were grown.

Also, truth be told, not every day was a bad day with Josh. I enjoyed his company when he was in a good mood. I liked us doing things together as a family when nothing set him off. The problem with Josh was he had more bad days than good days, and his bad days were very, very bad days. In my marriage, there were twenty-four-carat bars on the doors and windows, but it was still an ice-clad prison in Siberia.

I vacillated back and forth, but I finally decided to stay with Josh and concentrate on getting as much of an education as I could while waiting for my children to mature. Even though I had saved a lot of money, I knew, from previous experience as a single mom, that it would run out quickly.

What I really needed was a good job, a career. Unhappy as I was, I stayed in my loveless, abusive marriage because I needed a stable home to raise my girls. *Even if they grow up seeing Josh treat me like this,* I comforted myself, *at least they'll have food to eat, clothes on their backs, and a roof over their heads. They are safe. I'll continue to provide as much protection as I can.* I never relaxed, and I couldn't believe it; even now, the clock never stopped ticking. Somehow, I never felt fully safe. I never felt like I could trust that my children were safe.

Why Josh stayed married to me, I had no idea. I didn't know if he loved me as I loved him when we first married. He'd been my knight on a white charger, my hero. Yet now, I only felt positive about how good he was as a father. But even though he was a good father, he would often berate me in front of my girls, which I knew could be emotionally damaging to them.

One day, Josh came home from work stressed out. It wasn't unusual. I noticed him watching me with a sneer on his face. I thought, *he's probably going to berate me the first chance he gets.* The girls were in the living room, and I was close by in the kitchen, getting a frozen dinner out of the freezer.

"You don't need to eat that," Josh snarled, striding angrily into the kitchen, still in his work clothes.

"I'm hungry," I said.

"No, you're not," he said contemptuously. "You eat way too much to be hungry. Put it back."

I opened my mouth to argue with him, but I saw that Danni and Shayna had turned around from the television and were now watching me and Josh with wide, frightened eyes. I put it back in the freezer and stepped out into the living room.

"Girls, could you go downstairs now for a little while?" I never knew how long Josh's verbal abuse would last.

His abusive treatment of me was being "normalized" for them, and I was worried they would grow up to marry someone like Josh. I knew I had to show them I could take a stand. Suddenly, I had a flashback to the first time I met Josh's parents and realized that my daughters could wind up living their grandmother's life. A life where they had no love or emotional support but were treated with contempt and kicked while they were down by their own husband. Afraid for my children, I changed inside, vowing to continue my education, not just to get my freedom but to set a good example for my daughters. *Whatever it takes, I'm going to nursing school.*

Josh was transferred to the Pentagon shortly after I was excommunicated from the church, and I quit my job at the strip club to move our family to the Washington, D.C., area. We packed up, sold our house, and were gone within ninety days.

Deeply depressed, I struggled terribly with my decision to stay with Josh for the sake of my girls and to seek a higher education. Some days, I felt like wringing my hands and pounding my head against the wall because I was so conflicted about whether I was doing the right thing. How was staying with Josh 'taking a stand' when the girls saw how he abused me every day? Sinking deeper and deeper, I felt hopeless until I could see no way out of my marriage. I wanted to be strong, but I knew I was weak. All I had wanted from the beginning of my marriage was Josh's approval and affection, but that didn't happen. Some days, I even gave up the thought of leaving him, not seeing any way out. Even if I succeeded, it would take me years to get my nursing degree, and I was living with abuse now, today.

In despair, I even gave Josh all the money I had made working as an escort and a stripper. When I offered it to him the first time, a look of guilt crossed his face as if he didn't dare take it after he had got me excommunicated. But when I offered it a second time, he took it. He smiled as he counted it, thousands and thousands of dollars in cash.

Keeping my face neutral, I watched him count the money, and I froze the scene in my mind as a reminder that any man that would take the money his wife had been given by other men in trade for sex was nothing more than a pimp. With all the gaslighting he subjected me to, I needed the reality of his taking my money to keep me sane. I wanted to have a weapon to taunt him with, to throw back at him, and watch him squirm the next time he started verbally and emotionally abusing me. My only defense against him was to attack his high opinion of himself. I wanted him to look in the mirror and see the face of a hypocrite, just like the Pharisees that Jesus likened to whitewashed graves—white and clean outside, but inside, full of filth and unspeakable things. My gut twisted, and I realized I was living my mother's life. It was the same pattern.

One night, on our trip north to D.C., we stopped at a small roadside diner off the interstate to eat. I ordered a hamburger and fries, but I couldn't eat it. It felt as if there was a rock in my stomach, a heavy, hurting weight. Nauseous, I wanted to throw up.

But here we were, living in the middle of our trainwreck, Josh, myself, and our two daughters. Danni was eleven years old, and Shayna was nine. We were sitting in a diner in late summer, traveling cross-country, moving to another state to live, and I was desperately yearning for my lost, young lover. I had cut Ned off. No phone calls. No contact ever again. It was as if he had died.

Josh watched my face while we were sitting at that table. He knew I didn't want to be there with him. He reached across the table and patted my hand—one of the few times he had touched me in years of giving me breadcrumbs. But I was too lost in grief to respond.

CHAPTER 10:

Running to Somewhere

"If the Mountain won't go to Mohammed, then Mohammed must come to the mountain."
—Turkish folklore

I looked at the letter, and my mouth popped wide open. *Does this really say what I think it said? Finally!* The letter said I was accepted into a nursing program starting next year in September. *After all this time, it's for real, then!* A knot grew and twisted in my stomach. It was not the program I had hoped for. Accepting this placement meant living away from home. The program I had hoped to get into, closer to home, had no openings. Still, it was my ticket out.

Wow, if I'm going to do this, for sure, it's going to be hard! It's going to be like climbing a mountain. I just hope nothing bad happens. There are so many things that could go wrong. I shuddered at the thought. *Should I take this chance?*

After our move to D.C., my goal was to attend nursing school so I could get my registered nurse's license and a well-paid job. I needed to complete two years of a nursing curriculum for an associate degree. This would qualify me to sit for a state exam, which, if I passed, would allow me to be licensed as a Registered Nurse (RN). With a career as a nurse, I hoped to finally have the key to the lock on my cage.

Luckily, I had finished all my pre-nursing classes and had incorporated them into a Bachelor of Arts in Administration and an Associate of Liberal Arts degree before we left Georgia to move to Washington, D.C. After arriving at our new home, I found out that there were no current openings in the nursing schools in D.C. or the surrounding areas. In fact, there were two-year waiting lists, with preferential entrance for state residents. Even if I put myself on the waiting lists, there was no guarantee that I wouldn't get bumped lower.

The Army moved Josh and my family every one to two years, so I had no idea where we would be reassigned next. *How the heck will I be able to stay in one place long enough to make it to the top of the waiting list? Even then, how will I be able to stay in the program for two years when we move again?*

I filled my time in D.C. by seeking to earn a Master's in Administration with a focus in Health Services. I felt driven to finish it before the military moved us again. There were times when I took classes both day and night at four different colleges in the same semester—even on different military bases in the D.C. area!

I left myself no time to even think. In fact, huge blank spots developed in my memory that year due to the colossal demands of the graduate program, combined with undiagnosed clinical depression.

Just as reading books as a child had distracted me from my crappy childhood, having to focus on difficult or new subjects in college kept my traumatic memories in check. My brain stopped yelling at me and went blissfully quiet when I was struggling to master a subject. I finished that two-year master's degree in a little over one year, right before the Army reassigned Josh to Minneapolis, Minnesota. Off we moved again. I tried enrolling in nursing school there, but again, there were no local openings.

I was incredibly frustrated and discouraged. It felt like my dream of becoming a registered nurse and stepping into my freedom was again out of my reach. *Am I never going to be free? How long can I keep running away from my life?*

I wondered if the pre-nursing classes I had taken in Georgia would allow me preferential entrance into their nursing school. I called the school and spoke to the registrar, and found that I did, indeed, have preferential entrance into the school. She also said that if I wanted, I could enroll in the next class of nursing students starting the following year in September.

What a hard decision! It meant I would have to move to Georgia for two years. Danni was thirteen years old, and Shayna was eleven years old. I would only be able to come back to Minnesota to see my kids during school holidays and the one summer break between the first and second year of school. Once again, I realized I couldn't raise my girls alone.

I sat down and asked both Josh and my mother to watch and take care of my sweet daughters while I was away from them, attending school in Georgia. Thankfully, both agreed to help me. My mom, looking more energetic, her face not so gaunt, had now recovered from her health issues. She was glad to be able to help me with the girls. The following year, in September, I loaded up my little car, said goodbye to Josh and my children, and drove from Minnesota to Georgia to move into the dorms at the college.

I had never experienced going away to college as a young, single adult and living in the dorms. Now, as I drove across the country as a thirty-one-year-old, I wondered what my life in Georgia would be like. *Is this going to be two years of hell on earth?*

Having married at seventeen and given birth to my first child at nineteen, I had spent most of my adult life worried about how I was going to feed and clothe my children. I had no idea what it would be like to hang out with young, single adults with no responsibilities to anyone except graduating college. This would likely represent the majority of my fellow classmates. *Will I fit in with them and make some friends? Will I be alone for the next two years?* Compared to night classes on the military base, this would be a big change!

I was worried about being lonely, but once I settled into my scheduled classes, I made some friends. We all kind of hung out in a group. What was weird was that none of the people I hung out with were other nursing students. Since I was stuck in Georgia for two years, I decided to take full advantage of whatever the college offered in the way of any non-science subjects I was interested in. I enrolled in art, theater, and music classes whenever I could fit them into my nursing curriculum, and that's where most of my friendships came from.

Regretful and feeling guilty that I had to leave my children again, as if the separation when I was in the Army wasn't enough, I was determined to make the most of my time. What I didn't realize was that I was over-filling my time so that I would be too distracted to have flashbacks of my traumatic memories, which still tortured me as they had in Germany twenty-two years prior. They never really stopped. If I stayed busy, those flashbacks couldn't haunt me.

My daughters were older now. Danni was fourteen, in her first year of high school, and Shayna was in her second year of middle school. It was great to see Mom's health returned and reassuring to have her living with my kids and Josh while I was away at nursing school.

My marriage to Josh now consisted of two parallel, rarely intersecting, lives. Occasionally, Josh would say something cruel or abusive to me, and I would be reminded of how I never wanted to be under his thumb again. *Fool me once, shame on you. Fool me twice, shame on me.* So, even though I would sometimes consider reconciling with him because my daughters loved him so much, the fantasy of what I had once hoped our marriage would be would soon get wiped away by his abusive treatment. I wasn't angry so much anymore, but often disappointed when he wouldn't even make a small effort to treat me nicely.

I spent all my free time after nursing classes studying the arts and hanging out with all the artsy kids at the college, studying voice, piano, guitar, repertory theater, stage and set design, stage costuming, and more. Staying busy left me little time to ruminate over missing my children so much. Film art was my favorite class out of all the extra art classes I attended. In a trivia game our group played, someone would say a line from a movie, and everyone else tried to be the first one to guess which movie it was from and which actor said that line. I was pretty good at it because I was a heavy consumer of Blockbuster Video and Movie Gallery.

Of course, everyone in my group of friends planned to attend the up-coming Halloween dance because there's no holiday that an art or theater major loves more than Halloween. It's all about dressing up in costumes and drama! As might be expected, I daringly went *in costume* as a stripper. *Feelin' dang spanky!* I wore thigh-high, white, stiletto-heeled patent leather boots, a very low-cut white bustier, and a white, waist-high swimsuit bottom under an incredibly sheer, white-lace, gathered, calf-length skirt. I topped it all off with a white garter belt, a white feather boa, and white ribbons and jewels in my long hair. I was proud to be a dirtier version of Madonna singing, *Like a Virgin*, at the MTV Video Music Awards in 1984.

The night of the Halloween dance, I was walking with two of my friends, Dee and Hailey, in the college parking lot, gingerly stepping over the con-crete strips placed at the head of the parking spaces. Dee was dressed as a giant bumblebee, and Hailey was a scary but enticing succubus in black, torn, fishnet stockings, fangs, garter belt, and high-heeled, platform "Mary Janes."

Suddenly, our mutual friend, Randy, who was wearing a big trench coat, sneakers, and socks, ran over to us and surprised us by throwing open his trench coat. I'll give you one guess as to what his costume was. Short on cash, this was cheap. As Randy flashed us, I forgot to look where I was going, fell over one of the concrete strips in my stiletto heels, and twisted my ankle.

Even though my leg hurt badly, I wanted to go to the party and all the after-party parties. Still dizzy, I thought, *there's nothing wrong with me that beer or vodka can't fix.*

"Are you okay, Jade?" asked Hailey as she and Dee grabbed my arms and carefully helped me up from the ground.

"Get me about five drinks, and I'll be fine," I said as I limped across the pavement to a low wall and gingerly sat down to examine my leg. *Dang, it hurts!* Randy just stood there and looked dumbfounded. Sarcastically, I said, "Thanks for all your help, Randy. Great costume! You do you! I totally support that."

Looking down at my leg, I decided not to take off my leather boot to see what the damage to my ankle was because I figured the boot was probably holding my leg together, and boy, was I right! After everyone showed up, my whole wolf pack went to the dance, whooped it up, and then went to other parties off campus and whooped it up there, too. *So, this is what college life is really like!* We all got puking drunk that night, and my ankle didn't slow me down because, although I wasn't feeling *dang spanky* anymore, I wasn't feeling any pain, either.

I had a very difficult time taking my boot off later because my leg had swelled up in it. And after I took the boot off, my leg swelled up even bigger! My whole right foot, ankle, and leg up to mid-thigh had huge black and red bruises all over it. My foot was bruised almost totally black.

After I sobered up, I still didn't go to the doctor. *Who has the time for that?* I limped around campus for weeks afterward. It wasn't until years later that I realized I had probably broken a bone or two in my right ankle because the bone didn't heal right, and there was a bony knob on my ankle that hadn't been there before. *Duh!*

On my first summer holiday, I was so happy to load up my car and drive home to see my girls. I wanted to spend a quiet three months of summer with my precious girls, catching up with what they'd learned since I last saw them. I'd last seen them at Christmas break when we had celebrated Shayna's twelfth birthday. Not always succeeding in avoiding Josh, I tried not to fight with him. When it was time to drive back to Georgia to start my second year, I was tearful and upset over leaving my children again, but it was also a relief to not have to deal with Josh. One more school year to go— only nine months before I would be home for good!

One day, I was sitting in the cafeteria, waiting for my buddies to get out of their classes and join me for lunch, when an emaciated young man in baggy clothes, carrying a lunch tray, walked right up to me. I had never seen him before.

"Is this seat taken?"

I sized him up and said, "It's yours, have a seat."

We introduced ourselves and talked, getting to know each other. Soon, the others in my group started showing up and sat at the table with their lunches, too. It was funny, but just like that, Jerry became a part of our group, as if he always had been.

Several weeks later, I was walking around campus with Jerry after finishing our first afternoon classes.

"Jade, can you take me to the county health office one of these days?"

"Are you sick, Jerry?"

"I don't know, Jade, but I'd like to get tested for AIDS. I can't ask my parents to take me, and I don't have any money to go to the doctor."

"Sure, I'll take you."

"Thank you." He hung his head for a moment. "I've had a lot of unprotected sex with men, some a lot older. I'm a little worried about HIV."

"We'll go tomorrow," I promised, sensing the urgency of it. It took him a lot of courage to tell me those things. As he turned to walk away to his next class, I noticed he wasn't just skinny; he was skeletal, with hollow cheeks, temples, and eye sockets. His long limbs were thin and bony, and his pants hung loose and so saggy on him that they dragged under the soles of his shoes. When we first met, I saw that he was skinny, but now I looked at him with new eyes, missing none of the details of his appearance and searching for clues to his health. I had noticed that the food he ate never put any weight on him.

The next day, I took him to be tested and made a friend of the county health nurse who administered Jerry's AIDS test. When she found out I was a nursing student and lived in the dorms, she gave me a huge case of condoms to hand out at the college.

"Hand them out to everyone," she urged, fixing me with a long stare. I nodded and did exactly what she asked. It had been only five years since the battle against AIDS had started, and everyone was in danger. The nurse was really worried about the kids at the college. My nursing courses had given me enough education in this area to realize how dire AIDS was in our nation and across the world. It was a deadly epidemic, and people were dying everywhere. I handed out the condoms as if they were candy and made sure people knew how important it was to use them.

I took Jerry back about a week later to get his test results.

"Jade, I don't have AIDS! I'm okay!" he said happily, almost dancing out of the nurse's office.

But the nurse came out and, with a look, pulled me aside to speak to me privately.

"The test result could be a false negative. He could have HIV immunosuppression so bad that it could cause a negative test result, even if he actually has it."

She hesitated, pondering, her eyes downcast, deep in thought. "He looks sick. It's his extreme emaciation. He looks like he has AIDS to me." I nodded, and she went on. "Watch him and bring him back if anything further happens. He might want to get tested again in about three-to-six months."

"I will do so," I said.

I made sure that Jerry had a *lot* of condoms and that he never ran out. He would tell me excitedly when he was going to meet someone. He talked about his dreams of finding someone with whom he could fall in love and who would love him back, which is the same thing that I knew we all wanted.

Jerry and I lost track of each other after he finished his classes at the end of the semester a couple of months later. He left and I never heard from him again. I often wondered what happened to him and hoped he was happy and well. As a human being, Jerry stuck with me, as did his condition. It made me think more needed to be done in this arena. Maybe caring for those who had AIDS would be part of my nursing specialty. I wasn't sure, but the snapshot of Jerry's wistful face was deeply etched into my memory, and the care and compassion I felt for him never left.

Occasionally, my friends at the college and I would all pile in a car and drive to the gay bars in the nearest big city to drink and dance. Although there was no one I was involved with, I realized more and more that I was attracted to females as well as men and decided to accept who I was and go public with it. It seemed that many of my fellow college students were exploring their identities and discovering who they were. Maybe this was one of the growth processes in becoming an adult that young people dealt with in college when they were finally out from under the supervision of their parents.

Inspired by their bravery, I came out as a bisexual/lesbian to my college friends. I joked with my straight friends that I had access to 100% of the options for a partner, whereas they only had options for 50% of the population.

This was the early 1990s, in the first decade of the worldwide AIDS epidemic, and before the multitude of HIV drugs had been developed that we have today. One night, I stood at the edge of the dance floor at a gay bar, watching people dance and scanning the club for my friend, who had gone to get drinks for us. I spotted a very thin man walking unsteadily around the club, and my nursing classes kicked in. I went over to him to see if he was okay. He looked like he might be ill.

"Are you okay?" I asked. "I'm Jade. Do you need me to help you sit down?"

"Thanks," he said as I sat him down and leaned in close so I could hear him over the music.

"I'm Terry," he introduced himself, then paused. "I came here to see my friends, but none of them will talk to me."

Terry jerked his head to the right, drawing my attention to a man sitting at a table a little way from us, watching us. "You see him? He won't even talk to me. He pretends he doesn't even know me." I watched as Terry choked up and said, "We were friends for a long time, but not anymore. I've got AIDS, and now he doesn't even want to say hi to me."

I patted his back and put my arm around his shoulders. "Forget him. I'll talk to you." As a student nurse, I knew I couldn't catch HIV from him unless I encountered his body fluids. You couldn't catch HIV from a hug, but still, Terry was startled when he felt my arm around him. He was so thin; I felt his shoulder and backbones like knobs under my arm.

"It's been a long time since anyone wanted to touch me," he admitted.

I knew what that felt like. A surge of compassion flooded me. Then, a fire.

Angry, I scowled at Terry's "friend," who was still stealthily watching us. He cowered away from my glare.

My other friend returned from the bar, carrying two drinks, and the three of us talked for a while. Later, while I was out on the dance floor, I saw Terry get up and walk over to his "friend," who was still sitting at the table, watching him. As Terry approached, the man got up and hurriedly walked away. Terry just stopped and looked down at the floor, shaking. Then, he sadly wandered off somewhere, and I couldn't see where he went. I never saw him again, but it was another story, another human's pain—a ghost that would haunt me.

I was the oldest student living in the dorms, I think, although there was at least one other dorm resident close to me in age that I knew of. I probably would have been more comfortable in an apartment off campus, but I didn't want to deal with the hassle of having my own apartment. My sole mission was to go to school and graduate. I ate in the dining hall and slept in the dorms. It was easy to roll out of bed and head off to class five minutes before class started. I was saving time and money, and it felt great to maximize my sleep hours.

Over those two years, I got the full experience of attending nursing school and all the demands that went with it. It's a good thing I enjoyed my classes because it made getting good grades a lot easier. When I was missing my girls and I ached for them, time seemed to drag, but suddenly, I was close to finishing. I didn't know how to feel about that. After two years, I had a lot of mixed feelings. *What is it going to be like to be back home in Minnesota? How am I going to handle dealing with Josh on a daily basis again? Thank goodness, I will be with my daughters again! Thank you, God!*

I headed straight home to Minnesota, not bothering to attend the graduation. Instead, I had the college mail me my diploma. It had been hard to make the decision to go to nursing school, but I had completed my degree. It was done, and the stress and anxiety of it all was in the past. The most glorious part was to be reunited with my sweet children. They took it all in stride, but I never took being with them for granted.

CHAPTER 11:

Birthday Party

"If I never met you, I wouldn't like you. If I didn't like you, I wouldn't love you. If I didn't love you, I wouldn't miss you. But I did, I do, and I will."
—Anon

I did it! I squealed inside. I passed my state board exams quickly and easily, and I felt ecstatic. Finally, I could start working as a registered nurse. I was so relieved to finally show my daughters that I was working hard in a good career and could be a positive example to them. Also, now I could support them if something bad happened. Although they didn't know I had once worked as a stripper, I hugged myself with the thought that I didn't have to work in such a dangerous place anymore. All the effort and all the years were worth it. Something inside of me unwound for the first time since I'd lived in New Mexico. I had some breathing room to relax and feel confident and secure.

My first job was in a nursing home, working with elderly and disabled patients. Both nervous and elated on my first day at work, I was eager to do well at my job, plus make a difference in my patients' lives. As the weeks and months flew by, I settled into the routine of my career, quickly discovering that certain residents of the nursing home became my favorite patients.

Unlike a hospital with a high turnover of patients, I got to see the same patients every day and understand their personalities, their quirks, and their preferences. It was also easier to spot if something went wrong with a patient because I was the first to see if they were headed for a medical crisis when their behavior changed.

I particularly enjoyed taking care of one little old lady called Anna. She was everybody's idea of the sweet little grandma with white hair and rosy cheeks. One day, almost a year after I started working at the nursing home, I went into her room to give her the usual meds and found she had passed away. Just the day before, in the dining room, I'd smiled as I was handing out meds to the patients because I'd seen her sitting at a table in the corner, gobbling her dessert of strawberry shortcake with whipped cream.

Hmm, I thought, *that must be good!* I was happy she was enjoying her cake. I discovered that many patients would enjoy a last hurrah, as if their bodies instinctively knew that it was time for one last rally. Although I was sad that she had passed, I liked to think the staff had made her life as happy as they could while she was there in the last year of her life.

Mr. Walters was another favorite. An old black man, he was almost completely blind because of advanced age and various health problems. On my first day with him, I made the mistake of giving him too many pills to swallow at one time. Ooh, he complained fretfully to me about it! He wasn't rude, just stating his needs, and I was careful to give him his pills one at a time thereafter.

Each day, Mr. Walters was always very forthright when he talked to me, and I liked his direct manner. I noticed quickly that many elderly people really don't care what other people think about them. They are who they are, flaws and all, and if you have a problem with that, well then, it's *your* problem.

As I continued my job, I found there was something very inspirational about people who have lived a long life and have come to an acceptance of who they are, what their life has been and is now, and are at peace with themselves about it. That was a goal I set, and I hoped to achieve one day.

One morning, while I was at home by the kitchen door, getting ready to head off to work, Josh walked into the room.

"I don't like it that you're working," he blustered, "because it puts us in a higher tax bracket! We now have to pay more taxes."

My mouth dropped open, and I just stared at him, speechless. I thought, *what the heck? Are you kidding me? After all that everyone in the family has been through to help me get my nursing degree?*

I didn't say a thing to him; I just walked out the door to my car and drove off. It was useless to even argue. Now that I was back in Minnesota, living with Josh and my children, my goal was to keep my distance from Josh and not fight with him.

Nevertheless, as I drove, I realized what he said could be true. After all, he was the one who did our taxes; I knew absolutely nothing about it. Josh didn't like that I could control my own money now, but we still filed our taxes together as a married couple because we got more tax breaks.

Still, all the way to work, I was fuming with anger. *Thanks for the scowl on your face, Josh, and the nasty attitude. I mean, what else am I supposed to do but get a job? Thank you for devaluing all the work and struggles to achieve my RN.* I guess I shouldn't have expected anything else from him. I took a big breath and consciously lowered my speed and my heart rate.

Remember, Jade, what he thinks doesn't matter anymore!

After I started my job as a nurse, I was more easily able to enroll in another nursing school close to where I lived to complete my bachelor's degree in nursing. There was less competition because most nurses settled for their two-year associates and stopped advancing their education.

To my delight, there were no problems enrolling in the program, and there were plenty of available openings. It would still require hard work, but I had so much energy, and now I got to enjoy my girls whenever I wanted. That was a great boon.

Furthermore, I was planning to advance my education beyond my BSN by finishing prerequisites in three possible directions: one, a master's degree to become a nurse anesthetist; second, to become a physician's assistant; or the third option, to become a physician by going to medical school. *Climb that mountain! How far could I go? What new worlds could I conquer?* Even if I failed, I would learn a lot, and I realized it might be the experience of a lifetime.

As far as I knew, I had nothing to lose. I knew my plans would require almost infinite amounts of time and effort, but I reasoned, *it's not as if my life is so perfect and happy. I'll rest when I'm dead.*

I decided to climb the hardest, highest, most demanding mountain to strive to become a physician, and as a thirty-four-year-old, I zeroed in on completing my pre-med requirements and enclosing them in my four-year nursing degree. My goal was to apply to medical school, but it was rolling the dice for timing to get into medical school. Competition for the coveted slots was fierce.

After I applied, I had another decision to make. I took the plunge. I came out as bisexual/lesbian to my mother and Josh. My mother took it well and didn't treat me any differently, but Josh just rolled his eyes and changed the subject. *Nice! Thank you again, Josh. There is absolutely no point in talking to you, ever.* I didn't know why I still, at times, held fragments of hope for our marriage. It would never work when there was not one iota of respect from him in any capacity. I didn't know why I set myself up, but something in me knew that a loving, vibrant marriage was possible—if both parties wanted it and were willing to do the work.

Committed to getting involved in the LBGQ community I now identified with, I wanted to actually *do* something, whatever I could. It continued to be heartbreaking to hear of all the loss and suffering of those affected by the AIDS epidemic. I wanted to raise awareness or work with people and families affected by the disease.

To begin with, I decided to volunteer at an AIDS hospice. I told them I would do whatever they needed: mop the floors, run errands, clean toilets, go to the grocery store, whatever was required. There was something beautiful about providing service. I tucked my ego, fears, and desires away to serve someone else, and it didn't feel demeaning at all. It was empowering.

It was at the AIDS hospice that I met Sharon. She was a patient in her early thirties of Native American Indian descent with big brown eyes and long, straight black hair. I don't know how she caught HIV, but it had developed into full-blown AIDS. She had been diagnosed a while back and had been going downhill steadily at about the time when I met her.

Every couple of weeks, Sharon and I would go for a drive in my car to a park, walk around, sit on one of the park benches, and spend some time together, talking. It was good for her to get out of the facility and not stay cooped up inside all the time. I loved seeing Sharon's smile as she looked off to the horizon, watching the sunset, quietly happy as the wind blew her hair softly around her face.

Life got busy with getting the girls ready for back-to-school and other personal things at home, and I took a little time off from the hospice. A couple of months later, I read in the newsletter for volunteers that Sharon had died painlessly and peacefully in her sleep. I set the newsletter on the table, deeply and profoundly upset by Sharon's passing. Even though I knew AIDS had been winning the war over her body, it still came as a shock. It seemed so wrong that she had died. Along with Jerry and Terry, it was Sharon, primarily, who put a human face to the AIDS epidemic for me.

One day, after I'd gone back to volunteer at the hospice, a meticulous, black gay boy named Todd, a patient, asked me to run to the store for him. His friend, a nun, Sister Mary Catherine, was celebrating her birthday. Todd had tasked someone with getting a small cake and a birthday card for her, but the card wasn't as artistic or special as he wanted to give her. He asked me to go to an artsy gift shop close by and find a special card for his friend—something different.

I rushed out for this last-minute errand, as the party was scheduled to begin as soon as I got back. I quickly selected a card and brought it back to give to Todd.

Todd read the card, and his eyes bugged out. "Uhh, we're going to have to use the other card," he said, stunned.

I took a closer look at the card and realized I had been completely unconscious of who the card was for. It had a photograph of a very fat woman with a rubber belt around her waist attached to a machine that jiggles her fat, a device that was popular for weight loss in the 1920s. The inside of the card read, "Sorry, I may not have got you the vibrator you wanted. Have a

Happy Birthday anyway." Red surged up my neck to the top of my head, inflaming my face.

"I'm sorry, Todd. I guess I got the wrong card," I admitted ruefully, silently berating myself for being so stupid and wasting his money. *What the heck was I thinking? He said to get something different, not something inappropriate!*

"It's okay, Jade," Todd said. Then, he started to giggle a tiny bit before putting his hands over his mouth. He choked once or twice, making a strange sound in his throat, and I stared at him in concern. I thought maybe he had somehow got something caught in his airway as his eyes bulged out, but then he started laughing so hard the whole house heard him! Gasping and howling, he bowled over in his bed, holding onto his stomach, out of control. I backed out of the room, scared from causing such a commotion, and went downstairs. I apologized to the manager and told her I would reimburse Todd for the cost of the card. I could still hear Todd howling and screaming with hysterical laughter upstairs.

"Are you kidding, Jade? Do you hear him?" she chuckled. "This is going to be legendary! It's good for him to laugh. He needs to laugh more! It will help him fight off the virus."

We had a bit of a delay waiting for Todd to get ahold of himself, but we set the table and put the cake on it with some forks and plates in time for Sister Mary Catherine to arrive. An elderly, gray-haired woman in her nun's habit and sensible shoes, I watched in trepidation as all the staff wished her a "Happy Birthday." When Todd arrived, we sang *Happy Birthday* to Sister Mary Catherine and started cutting the cake.

Despite my *faux pax*, I couldn't resist. I leaned forward over the table and, in my best Jack Nicholson impersonation, smirked at the birthday girl.

"Sister Mary Catherine, I would bet that you have a *wild* side to you!"

Todd gasped, choked, snorted, and clenched the table with both hands for control.

"Oh, no, Jade. Don't get me started again!"

Sister Mary Catherine, smiling demurely, looked down at her hands in her lap and folded them, pleased, her cheeks turning pink at my compliment.

Despite the levity and humor that I consciously or unconsciously brought to these situations, I would never forget a single face of any of my patients… not the ones dying from AIDS, nor any of the little old ladies or men who touched my heart and soul. Similarly, I would never forget the frightened young women who were my patients at the women's free inner-city clinic where I also volunteered. I hoped I could be the kind of person who could bring light, kindness, and compassion in what could be a very dark world.

CHAPTER 12:

Heartbreak World

"The heart was meant to be broken."
—Oscar Wilde

I nervously walked into Club Astro, the neon sign for the gay club in Saint Paul sizzling overhead. I didn't know if I could be comfortable in such a place so close to where we lived. It was one thing to frequent clubs with college students out of state where I was going to school, but another thing to visit one in the twin cities, so near our home. Frantically, I searched for a place to sit that felt somewhat safe and not awkward.

And there he was, sitting at the bar, dressed in drag, every hair in place, his makeup flawless, looking incredibly beautiful.

I took a seat at the bar, several seats away from him, and ordered a drink. It was a lazy Friday afternoon, around 4:00 p.m., too early for the crowd to seep in. Besides the bartender, this person, and me, there were just a couple of other people playing a game of pool on the other side of the room.

The slanting afternoon sun shone jaggedly through the glass doors of the club, picking out the dust motes swirling in the air. I had deliberately gone to the club early, hoping to get my bearings before the main crowd gathered and swallowed me into its anonymous mass. Nervous about my new presentation to the world as gay, I was trying to find acceptance with others like me. I didn't want to feel alone anymore.

I was too shy to speak to anyone at first, but the beautiful man smiled at me, and after a while, he initiated a conversation. James was warm and welcoming, one of the most empathetic people I had ever met. We talked about everything. I was astonished to find that James was actually interested in who I was; he wanted to know everything about me. Later, I understood that this was why most people loved James. He genuinely loved other people.

We talked for hours as the bar filled up, the noise rising around us and forcing us to move closer on adjoining bar stools to hear each other. Over the following weeks, James took me under his wing and introduced me to everyone at Club Astro. I felt welcomed and accepted by the crowd, and I ended up spending most weekends at Club Astro. They became my friends.

Two years later, James and I were sitting together, laughing and enjoying each other's company. It was a crowded night at the club. James crossed his enviable long legs in his black patent leather stiletto heels and tugged down on his black micro-mini skirt. His long black hair fell over his shoulders as he brushed the silky tendrils back with his ringed fingers, its stick-straight strands falling to his slender hips. His black leather jacket had the right amount of grunge, a *je ne sais quoi* that said without words, *I don't give a crap what you think.*

I quietly smiled, looking at him, loving him, thinking how lucky I was to have him as a friend. James was a good friend to most people. He liked strangers to call him Jessy. "Jessy with a 'y', please," he would say airily when he dressed as a woman. But his closest friends were always allowed to call him James, no matter how he dressed that day.

James performed in the Drag Queen shows at Club Astro, looking just like Cher in her heyday. Whenever he lip-synced to the star's songs, he always pulled in a crowd. He looked hot, *really hot!* I knew a ton of women who would commit murder if they could somehow have his beauty. There was a power in that beauty—the kind of beauty that makes a man weak.

Tonight, James and I were sitting at a table for two, drinking and smoking cigarettes and catching up with each other on the events of the week. James was a kind person, endlessly kind, like his legs were endlessly long. Sitting at that table, cozily chatting, we could have easily been mistaken for a lesbian couple, two high femmes, except for James' 6 '4" height and his bulging Adam's apple.

Just then, a fifty-ish man with white hair, dressed in a dark business suit, approached our table, looking at James with admiration.

"Would you like to have sex?" he asked.

James leaned back in his chair and looked at him languidly with his dark, sultry eyes. He slightly tilted his head to the side and slowly smiled, the most beautiful vision in the room.

"No, thank you," James replied, still smiling.

Dazzled, the man smiled back at James, walked away, forgot where he was going, turned around lost, and then awkwardly found his way back to the bar.

My mouth had dropped open, and I was offended on behalf of my friend. Although James cross-dressed, he was straight, unlike me.

"Excuse me!" I said incredulously. "I can't believe he just propositioned you!"

James gave a dismissive wave with his hand, his rings sparkling in the dim light, inhaled a long drag on his cigarette, recrossed his legs, and breathed it all out.

"Yes, but he was very polite."

I was still in a loveless, sexless, heterosexual marriage with Josh. Neither of us went to church anymore. Alcohol helped me to deal with the pain of living in an emotional wasteland. His constant rejection of me was exhausting. How Josh was handling our bleak marriage was his problem. The old saying, "*You make your bed, and then you lie in it,*" applied to both of us now.

The part of my life that I lived identifying as a bisexual/lesbian woman had a pathos perfectly captured in the bittersweet lyrics and twanging riffs in the music I was listening to at the time, reflecting my life back to me.

Struggling to find the love and acceptance I craved, I knew I was not alone. It was the same for many others in the gay community, outsiders forming their own group in solidarity instead of just hanging out, isolated, around the periphery of mainstream society.

However, marginalization had some advantages. I had always loved fashion, and almost everything I ever learned about clothes, shoes, hair, and style, I learned from gay boys, drag queens, and Tom Ford. Lesbians, not so much, since I wasn't into a "Truck Driver" fashion aesthetic.

At Club Astro, I noticed three types of gay women—the truck drivers, the androgynous, and the high femmes. I was a high femme, which was a very feminine bisexual or lesbian woman, indistinguishable in a social setting from a straight woman.

Somewhat to my surprise, I found out that not everyone who hung out at the club was gay. Sometimes, straight people went there with their gay friends or family members. There were a lot of straight women who used to hang out at Club Astro, perfectly amiable with the gay men they interacted with. Maybe they just wanted to go to a bar where they didn't have to worry about getting hit on by men. Maybe a gay bar was the only place where men didn't treat them as a piece of meat.

Bisexual women like me were looked down upon by lesbian women. We were considered fence-sitters. *Make up your dang mind, Raylene! What's it gonna be? Men or women?* I waffled back and forth between identifying as a bisexual woman or a lesbian, even though I wasn't having sex with a man at that time. Although I was still married and living with Josh, I was off doing my own thing when I wasn't taking care of my kids and counting down the days for them to graduate from high school. It felt important to me to help them settle strongly into college and adulthood–things that I didn't have until so much later in life. Enjoying an active dating life with lots of women, I used to joke that monogamy was a dark wood that you polish.

In the middle of a sexless life at home and dating multiple women, I was earnestly working on healing some of the deeper issues of my life. Even though I wasn't going to church, it didn't keep me from praying to God for guidance at times, especially when early memories would hit me from out of the blue. I wasn't staying busy enough to keep them completely at bay.

I began participating in a hand-picked support/therapy group for incest survivors. Our therapist was finishing her doctorate degree, and as part of the requirements for her degree, she was collecting data and researching the effectiveness of different therapy techniques, some of which she had developed herself.

There were seven of us in the group initially, but one woman dropped out as the therapy continued over time. We were all women, both straight and gay, gathered to talk about our childhood experiences and how those experiences had shaped our lives, leading many of us down destructive paths and roads. It seemed that many of the pivotal choices each of the women had made in life stemmed from those damaging childhood experiences. We were our own worst enemies, dealing out pain and self-destruction. How can you overcome the enemy when the enemy you face is yourself? It was not easy work, and I often felt anxious before a session. This was when my prayers were the strongest, to get me to those sessions! *I can't do this on my own, Father!* I prayed, sometimes desperately, for peace of mind as I tried to make headway in my healing.

I often felt better afterward, but not always. Sometimes, the therapy increased my anxiety and left me less able to cope with the everyday problems and challenges that most normal people take in stride. We met once a week for six months. Not all of us were able to meet with the group every week, but we were mostly there for each other and formed friendships outside of our therapy sessions.

In therapy, I learned a lot about myself and my early childhood, including some incidents I had "remembered to forget." Although I remember more than enough to give me nightmares and flashbacks, I still have black holes in my memory, where my mind, mercifully, will not let me through to the other side. These memories are like a long, dark hallway of very tall, closed doors stretching out before me into infinity, disappearing into the past and murky shadows. *Do I really want to know what's behind those locked doors?* My unconscious mind has protected my conscious mind from remembering the details of these experiences.

I've had incidents of breakthrough memories for most of my life during times when I am quiet and my mind is unoccupied with work. These are incidents of PTSD (Post-Traumatic Stress Disorder) in which I am outside of myself, watching myself, and hearing myself say aloud, "Oh, he did that to me!" Then, the next moment, what I remembered would be erased, and I would be left looking into a black hole that swallowed up all thought and feeling, leaving me blank and numb. Although the therapy helped me to come to terms with these incidents, in the sense that I am calmer and more accepting of it happening now, it did not cure me.

One of the members of our group, Christie, was a thirty-something with medium brown curly hair to her shoulders, average height, big blue eyes, and slightly overweight, having given birth recently. Looking like a normal, suburban mom, she was straight and married with three kids. I noticed she was an introvert and a people-pleaser, with a child-like energy and a docile, almost infantile way of carrying herself through the world. It was as if her persona had had its growth arrested, and her edges hadn't fully formed.

After getting to know her, I thought, *I hope she has a good husband,* because she seemed so very vulnerable. She reminded me of a peeled orange, which was not a good thing in this world. Most people needed a thick skin to shield them from harsh realities. Over the following weeks, as her story unfolded to the rest of us during the group sessions, I realized she didn't seem to have the ability to protect herself from manipulators, ongoing. My stomach fell. I knew all too well that people like her got eaten by the sharks of this world.

We all hung out with each other to grab lunch, dinner, or a movie for years after the support group ended, both as a group and paired off. Christie and I often got together. I would meet her at her house for pizza during the day when her oldest child was at school, and we would have a good time talking about everything. Other times, I would pick her up at night when her husband was home to watch her kids and take her with me to hang out at Club Astro. We would play pool and darts and watch the Drag Queen or Drag King shows.

Christie loved James after meeting him, but that didn't surprise me—James had that effect on people. People just loved him. I would run off to chat with someone I had seen walk into the club and come back to find Christie in 'girl talk' with James, discussing make-up, clothes, or hairstyles.

In October, we went to Club Astro for my birthday party. James, Christie, Alexis, Sarah, and other acquaintances we usually hung out with at the club were there for the party with their partners. James had brought his girlfriend, a beautiful woman with long, dark red, wavy hair. They made a striking couple. We were all drinking and had a great time. There was a Drag Queen Show that night, and James performed with all of us cheering him on. I took a photo of Christie and me goofing around and making faces at the camera. If only I had known what was to come. Four months later, something terrible happened.

··●··

"I don't want her buried without me," I said as I handed my friend and therapy groupmate, Sarah, the scissors. My heart was shattered, like a glass that had been accidentally dropped on the floor, leaving pieces that were jagged, sharp, and cutting, dangerous to walk close to.

We were sitting in a circle on the carpeted floor in a small adjoining room off the main viewing area in the funeral home, where services were to start shortly.

One of Christie's relatives peeked into the room. "We'll be starting the funeral service for Christie in thirty minutes," she said and left.

I took my tote bag and spread its contents out on the floor: cards, notepaper, envelopes, markers, scissors, pens, tape, and stickers.

"Here, if you want, you can write a letter to Christie, or make a piece of artwork, or draw a picture. We'll put it in an envelope and place it in her casket to be buried with her," I explained. They were all there for Christie. It was February. It was cold and icy outside, and in my heart.

Sarah was hesitant, so I reassured her again that I wanted her to do it. "Just cut off a lock of my hair here, at the back of my head, near my neck." The group of women watched as she cut off my hair and handed it to me. Curling the long lock around my fingers, I put it in the envelope with the Valentine's card I had bought for Christie. I added my beaded ankle bracelet that I never took off and sealed it in the envelope, too.

Her husband had called me on the phone to tell me she had killed herself. At first, I didn't believe him. And then, when I did believe him, I couldn't stop screaming. Shaking, I dropped everything and drove to her house as something heavy pressed down on my chest. I had to stop my car to remind myself to calm down and breathe.

When I got to her house, the authorities had already come and removed her body. Her family and relatives had gathered to support and protect Christie's husband and children. I met her mother for the first time, and I let out a sob when I saw her–she looked so much like Christie.

"Oh, *you're* Jade!" Christie's mother said tearily. "Christie talked about you all the time. You made her so happy in the last years of her life."

"Hi, Jade," said one of Christie's aunts. "You know, she loved you so much. You were her best friend. You made her so happy!"

As I heard variations of these comments over and over from different relatives whom I had never met, I felt worse and worse. I was screaming silently in my head, *why didn't she call me? Why didn't she ask me for help?*

Then, I met Christie's father for the first time. Reeling myself in, I silently vowed not to cause a scene in a family already suffering so much. I knew why Christie had killed herself.

Everyone in our therapy group would know why when they found out she was dead. The answer was standing in her living room. Her father, the perpetrator of her mental agony. She couldn't take the pain of her traumatic memories of the abuse she had lived through anymore.

Every day, she lived with nightmares and flashbacks. I had never told her privately that I knew what that was like. Her father had finally shut her up permanently. She could no longer accuse him of the things he denied doing. This was probably the first family gathering in years that he didn't have to face her accusing, blue eyes. I wondered if he was relieved.

Searching his face when I was introduced to him, I looked for something: regret, remorse, sadness, guilt. I saw none of these emotions in his face. Instead, his affect was polite, bland, and superficial. He had an almost child-like immaturity to his emotions, a lack of empathy and worry despite the tragedy.

Feeling sick to my gut, I knew I had never met a more self-involved, pathetic human being in my life. I was shocked by his apathy, and fire filled my gut.

Christie's two daughters, just two and three years old, were happily playing in the living room, too young to understand their mother was gone. I was furious that Christie's father's face showed the same level of unconcern as her two youngest children. I had desired to end the pain of my traumatic memories many, many times. I recognized how close I had come to taking the same path as Christie, but God had taken that desire from me with a miracle, reminding me that He loved me more than I had ever known possible and that He was with me every day of my life.

Please, Heavenly Father, take care of Christie! She's home with you now. I don't know if I can bear this pain. Please, give me the peace that surpasses all understanding. I need you. I can't fix any of this; I don't know how to fix it. Help me, please!

About six months later, in the summer, I was sitting at the bar with James at Club Astro. We were hanging out before his show was due to start.

"Where's your little friend?" he asked. "I haven't seen her in a long time. What's Christie been up to?"

"James," I sputtered, my heart falling, "I thought you knew. I'm so sorry. I told Sarah to call you. When you didn't show, I just assumed... I thought you didn't want to come."

"Come where, Jade?" he asked, now looking concerned.

"To Christie's funeral. She killed herself several months ago," I said.

James was about to flick his cigarette ashes into the tray, but he froze with his hand halfway to the bar top. A look of pain ran across his face, and his hand with the cigarette shook. He carefully placed the cigarette in the ashtray, the smoke from the lit end curling up to heaven.

"I wish I had known, Jade," he said quietly, leaning in to speak. Then, he leaned back, picked up his leather jacket, and walked out the front doors of the club.

I remained sitting at the bar, watching James' cigarette burning to ash. I heard people calling for James, asking where he was because the show was starting soon, but I said nothing. James didn't come back to the club that night. I just sat there, watching his cigarette burn all the way down, and then out.

It was several months before I saw James at Club Astro again. Walking into the club one night, I saw him performing in the Drag Queen Show, and I was happy he was back. I had been worried about him. After the show, James and I talked, and he spoke to me about the good memories he had of Christie and how much he had loved who she was as a person.

"I didn't know she was in trouble, Jade; I just wish she had talked to me," he said regretfully. "I know I could have helped her. If I had been able to talk to her, I know I would have changed her mind." He shook his head sadly. "I would have helped her through her pain. I would have moved mountains for her." His thoughts and feelings mirrored my own. *If she would have just told me, it would all be different now. I could have helped.*

I had some somber experiences and many amazing, joyful experiences at Club Astro, just like in life. I looked at life differently from that point on and didn't take it so much for granted, nor my own healing. I was grateful that James felt the loss of Christie as deeply as I did. It spoke a lot about his heart.

Sometimes, when I am quiet and feeling nostalgic, I think of a night at Club Astro when I watched a tall, willowy man dressed as Cher slink his catwalk out on the stage to perform. And I remember how beautiful he was. I think of James.

CHAPTER 13:

Lovers and Friends

"I always play women I would date."
—Angelina Jolie

As an artsy person, I admired beauty in all its forms: nature, paintings, sculpture, literature, poetry, music, fashion, architecture, and more. Even the logic inherent in physics and mathematics was beautiful to me, although I hated both subjects in school. Women were especially beautiful with their satiny, squishy bodies and the lovely fragrance of their hair. Their gentle, nurturing ways and the unselfish care they showed to others were very comforting to me.

I felt safe with women, safer than I often felt with men. Although I would learn that many men were unselfish, too, I found women more willing to make sacrifices for their loved ones. Too many men I'd known were very self-involved and did not care how their behaviors damaged the people around them. I would find some women like that, too, and I had to learn to be careful who I let into my life. And sometimes… I was that woman.

Over the next five years, I fell madly in love with three different women, who all played a remarkable role in helping me discover myself. I met Amanda through a "bisexual girl seeking bisexual girl" ad on a gay message board. Maybe not a good idea from a safety standpoint, but she was fabulous.

Amanda and I agreed to meet at the bar, Ruby Tuesdays, one afternoon, and she showed up with her long legs and lithe body gift-wrapped in black leather. *So hot!* After I put my eyes back in my head, I noticed all the guys in the room watching us closely. They must have figured out that we were on a date. Amanda and I left the bar early to go to a more private location. We enjoyed ourselves for a time, but we were incompatible in many ways. I discovered this one day when Amanda came over to my apartment to hang out after I finally left Josh. Freedom! I was living in my own apartment and working as a nurse, even though Josh and I were still legally married. Amanda started thumbing through the books on my bookshelves while I was in the kitchen, preparing some drinks and snacks for us to eat while we watched a movie.

"Why do you have all these cheap books, Jade?" she called out from the living room.

"They're classic books, Amanda," I replied as I returned to the living room carrying the tray of snacks. I pointed to the titles on my used paperback copies of books by Thomas Hardy, Emily Bronte, Jane Austin, Homer, Ayn Rand, Mark Twain, and others. I was working my way through the older classics to more contemporary classics to continue my grounding in liberal arts.

"But they look cheap," she sneered. I raised a brow.

"Yes, but the words are the same, Amanda, no matter whether they're enclosed in paper or leather binding," I said a little defensively. "Plus, I can afford to buy more of the books I want if they are in paperback."

Amanda just rolled her eyes, and I stiffened.

I like beautiful things as much as the next person, but economics was always a fact of life. Amanda liked expensive things; she especially liked the perceived status that came with owning expensive things. I had recognized a long time ago that you can't have everything you want, but Amanda didn't want to deal with that fact. That's when I knew our relationship wouldn't go the distance. It was readily apparent that Amanda was looking for someone to give her the lifestyle she felt she was entitled to.

I was working as a nurse while waiting to hear back from the med schools I'd applied to, but I was not swimming in money. Amanda didn't like waiting for a more prosperous day. She expected me to pay for everything now when we went out.

Amanda worked as a salesclerk at an organic food grocery chain, and for someone who worked with a lot of tree huggers, she was really into an elitist lifestyle. She drove a very expensive gas-guzzler. *Whatever happened to saving the planet by reducing our carbon footprint?* Amanda seemed to be doing her best, however, to reduce her dependence on our capitalist monetary system. One day, she presented me with some supplements and said they were mine. I was bewildered.

"Thank you, Amanda. That's very thoughtful of you, but I don't need these. Why are you giving them to me?" I asked, confused.

"Jade, do you know how hard it was for me to get these?" she said angrily.

"I guess I don't," I uttered, completely clueless.

"I just want you to know that we're square now. I owed you forty-five dollars, and here it is," she stated with finality, handing me a container of organic, plant-based protein powder and a bottle of marshmallow herbal extract.

Finally getting a clue, I realized that instead of giving me the money she owed me in cash, she had stolen expensive items from the store she worked at to pay me back.

A couple of weeks later, I woke up one morning after a night out with Amanda to find myself alone. As I scrambled to get dressed and make sense of the black hole that was my memory of the last twenty-four hours, I found at least ten phone numbers on separate little pieces of paper in my jean pockets. They flew out like confetti when I picked up my jeans from where they lay puddled on the floor from when I took them off the night before and shook out the wrinkles.

My head was hammering after a night of way too much alcohol. When I called Amanda on her cell phone, she screamed at me for being a jerk, and then abruptly hung up. I had no memory of what had happened the night before, and Amanda was too pissed to tell me.

Several days later, when I went to Club Astro, about a dozen women came up to me all night to continue conversations I didn't remember having with them. I must have flirted with a sizable number of women at the club the night I had no memory of.

Oh my God. I blacked out. That has never happened to me before.

Amanda and I broke up because I was a major jerk. I regretted my actions, but I wasn't completely heartbroken when Amanda and I parted. Realistically, I knew I couldn't compete with all the wealthy men out there who were anxious to take her out to expensive restaurants and buy her things.

My relationship with Amanda highlighted that I had a drinking problem. This worried me. Deep down, I knew I was hiding again, and I knew I needed to quit.

It would take me years to get my drinking under control, but it improved gradually as my life circumstances changed for the better. My unhappiness about feeling unloved and unwanted in my marriage to Josh played a big part in my drinking excessively. I was able to finally get control of it after Josh and I divorced. But it took a long time because drinking had become a habitual pattern of behavior that I depended on to manage my moods. It took years to build new habits, but I finally stopped drinking regularly. Amanda was a major catalyst in helping me know I needed to change. In the meantime, I had more growing and learning to do.

Reba, an androgynous lesbian with short blond hair and blue eyes, worked for Canon as a sales rep. We met when she asked me to dance at Club Astro one night. One look, and I was a goner. I went home with her that night. When I woke up in the middle of the night to go to the bathroom, I stopped, amazed, on my way back to the bed, to just stare at her. I couldn't believe I was in bed with this incredibly beautiful woman. After I got back under the sheets, she stirred sleepily, partially woke up, and grasped my left calf, cupping it in her hand and holding onto it as if to make sure I was still there. Then, she fell back asleep.

Reba had her own story. As a young teen, Reba had been discovered kissing her girlfriend in a secluded area by some boys she knew from school.

"We were just innocent, Jade," she shared. "Neither of us knew what it meant to kiss each other."

Both girls were gang-raped by the boys to "punish" them for preferring girls.

As Reba and I grew closer, she used to make fun of me for being a high femme, but not in a mean way. She would tease me by handing me my bangles when we were getting dressed to go out at night.

"Don't forget your jewelry, Jade!" she would laugh. "Don't forget all your frou-frou!"

I wanted to be with her forever, but we both had our issues. The biggest was that she wasn't in love with me as much as I was in love with her. In addition, Reba was more attracted to other androgynous lesbians like her rather than high femme lesbians like me. I wasn't really her type. And there was nothing I could do to change that, no matter how much I loved her.

Another issue that came between us was my being bisexual and still married. Bisexual women are often perceived by lesbians as untrustworthy, having access to 100% of the options for a partner, male or female.

After we broke up, I thought about Reba for months, rehashing memories and trying to think of something I could have done differently. I was learning that you can't make a relationship work just because you want it to work, a lesson I thought I had previously learned from Josh! Evidently, the lesson needed to be repeated.

No matter what, I had learned a long time ago that you don't mess with someone's sexuality. Whatever people identify their sexuality to be, it's best to leave them alone with it to make their own decisions. I learned to love the person with no reservations and respect their agency to make their own choices.

People who were curious about a gay lifestyle sometimes approached me for sex. It was like playing with matches, so I always turned them down. It could be explosive, and you couldn't predict what would happen. They could have a meltdown afterward. I had witnessed too many meltdowns in our crowd.

I was at Club Astro one night when I was approached by a couple asking me for a *menage a trois*, a threesome, with them. They were a young, very attractive, wealthy-looking couple in their thirties.

"No, thank you," I said firmly, "but there are a lot of people here; I'm sure someone will be interested."

It wasn't the first or last time I was approached by someone with that offer. I rejected their offers for many reasons, the first being they were strangers. Going off somewhere with people you don't know for sex is a good way to wind up dead and buried in a shallow grave. Second, I didn't know whose idea it was. Whether coercive on the man's or woman's side, I wouldn't have any part of a coercive relationship. Third, if this was the first time for group sex for either of them, it was not for me! And fourth, I wasn't into men at the time, and that meant I had no interest in having sex with the man.

I drew a thick, black line between friends and lovers. When I met someone, I knew right away whether I wanted to be friends or lovers with them. In the past, I had friends who wanted to be my lovers, but I always said no. Christie once asked me if we could have sex. She was curious, but I turned her down. I enjoyed being her friend, and I knew how vulnerable she was from us spilling our guts in our therapy group. The direct purpose of our group was to find unselfish support and comfort from other women who had survived similar experiences with incest. It was not a place to hook up. We each had work to do on ourselves, and sex would have been a distraction and a complication neither of us needed.

James asked me once if we could be more than friends. We had a good friendship and compatibility that could have been the basis for a loving relationship. Although I loved him for the sweet, kind person he was, I was not into a heterosexual relationship at that time. James had just split up with his girlfriend with the gorgeous red hair, and I could tell he was hurting. I didn't want to be a rebound romance. I cherished him too much.

Later, James told me that his girlfriend had broken up with him because she had an eight-year-old son, and she was unsure about what kind of influence James' cross-dressing would have on her son as he matured.

She had decided to put her child first, even though it cost her James. I understood her decision. James understood, too, even though it broke his heart. The truth was, I found that living a gay or alternative lifestyle could often be much harder than a conventional life. No one wants to pile pain onto those they love. Every day, normal life hurts enough.

Ms. Hollywood Gorgeous, Alexis, looked like she had stepped right off a movie screen like one of those old-time movie stars. She had perfect features in a heart-shaped face with soft blue eyes and very thick, straight, ash-blond hair down her back. Alexis was bisexual like me. She had three children and was married to a man who lived separately from her in a different part of their big house. I never met him. He was often traveling for business. I don't know what his job was, but he was almost never there to count the number of nights I spent with her.

I'd first met Alexis in college, finishing my pre-med studies, and later ran into her at Club Astro. I thought it was a coincidence, but one night, after we had become a couple, she walked into the living room and stood in front of me as I was sitting on the couch.

"Jade, do you remember the first night we met at Club Astro?"

"How could I forget! I didn't know what to say to you, Alexis," I admitted. "You were so beautiful; I was kind of stunned. I think I just mumbled hi to you. I couldn't tell if you were there because you were gay or if you were hanging out with your gay friends. I was hoping you would let me ask you out, but didn't know."

"Yeah, you looked confused… and *interested*." She came over to me, sat at the other end of the couch, and put her bare feet in my lap. I started massaging them.

"I tracked you down because I wanted you," she noted gleefully. "I asked everyone I knew for information about you. I got *all* the dirt on you," she teased. "I found out that you hung out at the club and hunted you down 'til we could meet again."

"Wow! I've never had such a dedicated stalker before," I said playfully as I continued to rub her feet.

"So, Jade, have you figured out yet whether I'm gay or not?" She smiled at me, cat-like.

"Actually, I have figured that out, Alexis. Thank you for asking."

It was funny that whenever I would sleep over at Alexis's house, usually after a night out, I would wake up to find my socks gone. Her youngest kids would always steal my socks because Alexis didn't keep up with doing the laundry, and her kids suffered from a chronic lack of socks. I would always go home with bare feet inside my shoes.

Alexis and I were locked into the gay community in St Paul. We ran the HIV/AIDS hotline and education program at the college we attended, which was funded by a grant. At college fairs, we handed out pretty gift bags containing HIV safe sex education cards, condoms, and dental dams.

I had other volunteer activities, not involving Alexis, with other organizations. For example, I volunteered at a homeless, runaway teen shelter as a counselor for troubled teens. For many of these kids, the only alternative to our shelter was a cardboard lean-to under a bridge with a life on the streets as a sex worker. A high percentage of the homeless teens at the shelter were gay, many of whom had either run away or been kicked out of their homes because they were gay.

After first volunteering at the shelter, I was later hired as a paid staff member. As a registered nurse, I also worked with an organization that sent me to high schools to give talks in health classes on HIV/AIDS/Safe Sex. Additionally, I volunteered my time at a free, inner-city women's health clinic. I saw many women who were victims of domestic violence, and the abuse they suffered included financial abuse to the point where they were kept from having access to medical care. Finally, I was still doing volunteer work at the AIDS hospice. It was a lot of work, and I kept busy with my regular job as a nurse and with my volunteer work.

After a while, my hectic lifestyle finally caught up to me, wearing me out and leaving me craving for a more normal life—a quiet, boring life. I wasn't sure if I wanted to live a gay lifestyle anymore. *God, how I want to be bored!* My life was way too exciting and filled with far too much drama from the club and my friends. Plus, I was tired of battling dragons in my many volunteer jobs. My efforts to give back to the community and make a difference started to make me feel as if I were back in the Army at Fort Jackson, crawling up the sand dunes in Little Egypt.

Discouraged, I started to question myself. *Am I like Don Quixote, tilting at windmills?*

I was burnt out. Every day was a struggle as I worked to get accepted into medical school. Both my kids were in college, and although Josh and I were still married, we had lived separately for over a year.

I knew the stress would be cranking up once I started medical school, and I knew I needed to *uncomplicate* my time and my life. *How can I take responsibility for anyone other than my kids and myself? I can barely manage my own crap. How the heck am I going to be able to take care of Alexis?* No more promises, ever again, I decided, that I didn't know for sure I could keep.

So, I broke up with Alexis. I was traveling fast and alone, and I learned from my relationship with her that loneliness was sometimes a part of the journey. I wished things could have been different, but it was the only realistic decision I could have made. I didn't know that I was running from myself or running from God. I was just running.

After submitting my application for two years straight, I was still not accepted into medical school. Incredibly frustrated and stressed, I thought, *was all the work I've done to get my education for nothing?*

The clock was ticking. But it was different this time. My girls were as safe as their own choices allowed them. Now, it was ticking for me. I was getting older.

I took one year off and then applied again the following year. This time, in addition to all the medical schools I had previously applied to, I also applied to a medical school where the first two years were taught at a campus in the Caribbean, and the last two years were taught at hospitals back in the United States. I was accepted into that school and decided to go for it.

After being accepted, I had to get ready to move to the Caribbean. I would be forty years old when I started medical school! I was elated to have had a cheap, quick, uncontested divorce. Because Josh had been so generous with me and my girls by paying for my education and theirs, all I wanted from my marriage of over ten years was my personal possessions, like my clothes and my car. I felt so guilty for my part in the failure of our marriage. When I asked Josh for a divorce, I told him to get a lawyer, have the divorce papers written up, and I would sign them. I didn't take any money from him even though I was entitled to half of the property we owned, our bank accounts and investments, and even half of his retirement pay from the Army. I signed it all over to him. I took out student loans for medical school.

Working hard, I got everything in my apartment packed up, organized, moved, or given away several months before I was due to leave. My delicate China set and my wedding rings went to Shayna, and much of my furniture went to Danni. Thank goodness, both of my daughters were in college and needed things!

One day, Danni came over to my apartment to help me set up an email account to use in medical school. As we were working on the computer, we saw the news that the son of the late President John F. Kennedy was missing. John F. Kennedy Jr's plane had disappeared somewhere near Martha's Vineyard. Several days later, they found his plane, which had crashed, killing him, his wife, Carolyn, and his sister-in-law, Lauren. I was horrified at the waste of it all, a future denied to three vibrant young people. I thought of my mother's heartbroken reaction to his father's death almost forty years before, to another future denied, cut off way too soon.

This arbitrary tragedy made me realize, front and center, that I, too, might not have a future. It could be taken away at any minute.

I might not have another day, I decided, *so I'd better get serious.* I needed to follow the advice I'd given to Christie to not get distracted. It was time to get my act together.

CHAPTER 14

Welcome to the Jungle

"I have no special talents. I am only passionately curious."
—Albert Einstein

After arriving on the island of Dominica, I settled into my studies, working harder than I had ever worked in my life. Keeping my head down and in my books, I did my best to mind my own business and not get distracted because there was an endless amount of information to learn and memorize and never enough time to learn it all.

I was elated when I got through the first semester with good grades. It was a relief because now I knew I could do it if I worked hard enough.

That night, all the med students who had just finished final exams for the semester let off some steam. Someone hired a DJ and caterer for a block party in one of the nearby neighborhoods around the school. Most of the students were drinking like fish and dancing to the loud beats until two in the morning.

Some of the local islanders came out onto their balconies to watch us, amazed at our drunkenness and hellraising. They knew we were studying to be doctors and would one day make more money than they could possibly ever dream of. The people on the island were mostly very conservative

Christian people. It was a third-world country. Poverty and crime were common, with poverty mostly causing the crime. But most of the people lived their lives based on decent, moral principles. I saw many examples of lost wallets or purses being found and returned to students with all the money still inside them.

One spring day, I sat on a dusty, broken cement wall near a run-down pharmacy near my school. I spoke with an old island man I'd seen multiple times. We sat for an hour, his withered skin and lines of wrinkles often turning up in a contagious smile. This is what had made me curious about him in the first place. Every time I saw him, I couldn't help but think, *what is his story?* That day, I had enough courage to ask, and he told me all the reasons he was very satisfied with his life, even though I could tell that he had next to nothing—especially by the standards of my Western, first-world culture.

"God is good!" he exclaimed. "God provides for *all* His children!"

He gave me one example after another of the many blessings Jesus Christ had given him. The old man was so grateful. He praised God just for having basic items, like food, shelter, the clothes on his back, and his health, even though he didn't always have all those things, all the time.

This conversation radically changed my perspective on my life and had a lasting impact on me about how much Americans take for granted the privileges and abundance they enjoy every day. I'd once been incredibly impoverished and worried about my children, but it had been decades since I didn't have food or worried over their safety. The man stayed on my mind and gave me a different view to ponder. I had felt poor in med school, but from that day forward, I realized I was very blessed.

The medical school on the island reminded me of growing up in Hawaii, as it was also a big melting pot of cultures. We had students from all over the world and from all kinds of backgrounds. One Persian girl taught me how to make yogurt with a cooking pot and some towels. There were students from India, Russia, Ukraine, China, and Iran, to name a few, in addition to those from the United States. The basic requirements to attend the school were that you had to complete all your pre-med classes, pass your MCATS, and speak English because all the classes were taught in English.

Another girl, attending the medical school from Ukraine, asked me to be her girlfriend. Natalya had lived through the 1986 Chernobyl nuclear power plant explosion as a child and had survived thyroid cancer. Even though she was attractive—beautiful, slim, a natural blond with blue eyes—I turned her down. I had relapsed just once earlier in the school year, and I was determined not to go back to that lifestyle. I was staying away from women. I needed to concentrate on my classes and not get distracted. Occasionally, I dated men, deliberately trying to transition back into a heterosexual lifestyle. They didn't distract me as much.

The two years I spent on this island in the Caribbean were like trying to survive in a jungle. The island had its own jungle, a rainforest, in the middle of the region, but the real jungle was medical school. It was sink or swim, baby, and once again, I had to watch out for the sharks! The classes in anatomy and physiology, pathology, microbiology, surgery, obstetrics, pediatrics, and the rest were very intensive. I got up early every morning, studied before classes, attended said classes, and then studied after classes until I fell into bed at night. Rinse and repeat. Study groups helped with exams, but most of the work was done individually. Trying to make a dent in the copious amounts of reading and memorizing, I often fell asleep at my desk while studying into the wee hours of the morning.

A high percentage of the students flunked out. It was a higher percentage than most U.S.-based medical schools. Everyone stressed about the very real possibility of failing, which fueled the drinking and casual sex. These things were distractions, a coping mechanism for many of the students. Some girls got pregnant and married other medical students during school, and I couldn't imagine how much more difficult it would be to deal with morning sickness while studying for exams, doing labs, and taking tests. I also couldn't imagine the difficulty of caring for a baby as a medical student or even a medical resident without a lot of help from the baby's grandparents or a nanny. Thank heavens, I would not have that problem, as I could not get pregnant.

Another all-too-common story involved the stress of separation that caused a lot of break-ups or divorces. Many couples arrived on the island for one of them to attend medical school, yet within months, they would split. The partner who was not attending the school would leave and go back to the States.

A joke that always made the rounds of the first-year, incoming medical students was, "Get out of medical school *now*, before it's too late! Leave now. Otherwise, you're trapped for the rest of your life!"

This joke, like most jokes, was funny because it had some truth to it. The point was that if you attended medical school, you were trapped into being a doctor for the rest of your life—because there was no other way to pay your school loans off.

And... it could get worse. If you flunked out, you were *also* screwed financially for life because you would most likely not be able to find a job that paid a high enough salary to pay off your school loans. Your credit rating could wind up in the toilet.

I came to know many doctors over the years who hated their jobs but were stuck. They couldn't get out, either because they owed so much money that they couldn't leave or because too many people in their family depended on the lucrative income they made as a doctor. In other words, they were trapped into being human ATMs for other people, going to work every day at a job they hated.

Despite the joke and the reality, I felt 100% committed to medical school and my future. It was a good thing because anatomy lab could only be described as a rite of passage or a den of torture. It wasn't unusual for medical students to faint while cutting up dead bodies. Another joke among us was that there were two ways to get into medical school: get in as a med student or get in by donating your corpse. Yeah, it was a bad joke, but when you've been cutting up the same body for five weeks, and it's growing mold, jokes are sometimes all that gets you through. When your shoes are slip-sliding across the linoleum in the melted body fat that's dripped onto the floor, you can't get the smell of the formaldehyde out of your nostrils, your hair, or your clothes, and you feel like puking, well, then you know you have arrived!

Level 99, complete! You have crossed over to a new level. You have had an experience that only doctors and psychopathic killers share in terms of your intimacy with dead bodies. Your only solace is what you'll hopefully be able to do with that knowledge to save lives in the long run. It kept me going.

After completing my first two years of medical school in the Caribbean, I moved back to the United States. I was to train at several hospitals, first in Miami and then in New York City, to finish my last two years of medical school. In my third year, I was attending my surgery rotation in Florida and just happened to have a day off on Tuesday, September 11, 2001.

Even though I was off that day and would have loved a luxurious lie-in, I awoke early in the morning to an empty fridge. I needed to go to the supermarket to pick up some food. Arriving home to my sunny apartment, I put my groceries away and went into my bedroom to undress, eager to spend the day watching TV in bed, sleeping, and recovering from my twelve to thirty-six-hour work shifts.

Katie Couric was on the news, her voice and face strained. That's when I saw footage of smoke rising from one of the Twin Towers in New York City. Horrified, I thought, *is this an accident? How could this happen?* When the second plane hit the other tower, I knew that our country was being attacked.

What should I do? As reports came in from other crashes in different areas of the nation, I panicked for a moment and called the girls to make sure they were safe. Although I was scheduled to move to New York City in three months to start my clinical rotations for my last years of med school, there was nothing I could do right at that moment. I knew doctors in New York City would voluntarily go into the hospitals on their days off to help in this disaster. It was disheartening to know there was nothing I could do to help. So, I sat on the bed and watched the television, feeling useless and scared.

Later, a friend of mine, a medical resident living in New York City, told me what he experienced. Early that morning on 9-11, he was just starting his morning clinic at Kings County Hospital when the large television screens in the auditorium-sized waiting room were suddenly filled with those same scenes of planes crashing and all the ensuing chaos. All clinical appointments were canceled, patients were sent home, and medical staff rushed to set up triage stations outside the emergency room doors to handle the massive numbers of expected trauma victims. They waited all day... but other than first responders with eye and lung injuries sustained from fumes and concrete dust, no one else arrived. It was devastating to the medical personnel that nearly all the people trapped inside the Twin Towers perished. When I moved to New York City, several months later, the city was still shell-shocked. I settled into my clinical rotations, working hard, and the long hours left me no time to think about the tragedies. Slowly, the area at Ground Zero was cleaned and cleared, and the debris was sorted and taken away. As time passed, broken lives were awkwardly patched back together.

In January 2003, I started my orthopedics rotation. The Christmas holidays were over, and everyone was getting back into the swing of a regular work week with clinical and surgery schedules.

Fortunately, all was *not* doom and gloom with the orthopods, and I quickly discovered that the orthopedic residents were a close, fun group. I called them a "wolf pack," snapping and growling at each other but banding together at any outside threat.

There were four residents: Frank Cho, the chief resident, a short, serious Asian guy who looked like he was sixteen years old; Alan Oster, a Boston-bred quiet bear of a man; Tyrone "Ty" O'Hara, a tall Irish redhead who seemed to always be in a fight with someone; and finally, Paul Nero, a boisterous Italian, native New Yorker, with a filthy mouth only surpassed by his filthy mind. All four fought like brothers, not always agreeing and deliberately causing trouble for each other just to liven up the boredom of long hours and crushing patient caseloads. It cracked me up that all the ortho residents were tall men, 6' 2" and up–except for Frank.

The first time I saw Alan, he was getting dogged out for being late to medical rounds by Frank. That was a sight to see! I couldn't help cracking up every time I glanced up from my patient chart at the sight of a very tall, stocky man getting ripped by an Asian Doogie Howser.

A day or two later, I worked with Alan and Paul, doing surgeries. One was a hip fracture repair on a little old lady. When the surgery was done, Alan and Paul had to transfer the patient from the surgical table onto a gurney by interlocking their fingers under her to lift and move her so she could be taken to the recovery room.

"You got finga?" Paul asked.

"Yea, I got finga," Alan answered, deadpan.

That became the catchphrase for the rest of the residency between Alan and Paul, and at times for me, during the rest of my rotation through orthopedics. Whenever we would run into each other, instead of saying "Hi," we would say, "You got finga?"

All five of us welcomed the chance to smile and laugh because our work was so serious and stressful. I always loved helping people, but now we were dealing with matters of life and death. We had to bring our A-game to everything we did and every decision we made. It could wear you out if you didn't find opportunities to have a little bit of fun. Because of these guys, the orthopedics rotation in my last year of med school was the most fun I experienced in any of my clinicals.

A week or two after the 'finga' incident, I noticed Dr. Alan Oster staring at me. This time, it wasn't with humor. It appeared to be with interest.

What is up with that?

Walking into the call room early one morning, half a month later, I almost ran into Alan as he was coming out. In the middle of the doorway, we both stopped short, looking at each other, and he stared at me again, this time stunned like a deer in headlights.

I smiled at him and then scooted around him because he seemed unable to move.

I think he likes me, I thought.

CHAPTER 15

Paging Dr. Oster

"Men have only two emotions: hungry and horny. If you see him without an erection, make him a sandwich."
—Anon

I was keeping an eye out for a potential long-term relationship. Sex was all too easy to get if I wanted it, but I was looking for more than a booty call, which, considering my ultra-busy schedule, was a waste of my time. Bored with the singles dating scene, I wanted to build something real for my future.

Considering my ten years in a trainwreck of a marriage, I now wanted a man who was gentle and kind–the exact opposite of controlling and abusive. If I had the courage to get mixed up with a man again, he would have to prove to be loving and affectionate.

I started to get to know Alan during my orthopedics rotation, noticing that he had kind and beautiful hazel eyes that complemented his dark, curly brown hair. Watching him carefully with returned curiosity and interest, he seemed to check most of the boxes.

I wasn't sure yet. I had to be sure. He was introverted but interacted well with others in group settings. This was a definite plus for me because

I was socially inept a lot of the time, even if it wasn't always noticed by other people.

Alan had a quiet but happy, upbeat personality. He had none of Josh's moodiness or negativity. I didn't have to walk on eggshells around him. Although capable of critical thinking, Alan was not a critical person, and it was refreshing to see how careful, patient, and respectful of other people's feelings he was when he talked to them. I saw evidence of these traits during his interactions with patients and medical staff in the hospital. I started feeling a thrill each time I saw him. I was really hoping he was what he appeared to be. But I would have to *know*.

The primary character trait I was looking for in a potential partner was the ability to care for someone other than himself and to be unselfish enough to sacrifice something *he* wanted for the sake of another person. That other person did not have to be me, but I had quickly grown tired of the arrogant, often narcissistic doctors—male and female— I ran into daily. These doctors were as prickly as porcupines defending their territory, standing high on their egos, elevating themselves above the rest of the common folk, and demanding that others treat them as if they were God Almighty.

One afternoon, I met a doctor working in the ER who I had never met before. He lacked no confidence as he leered at me and licked his lips suggestively when I happened to make eye contact with him. *So gross!* Evidently, he was able to multitask by dispensing medical care to his patients while leering at his co-worker, *Moi,* as I was trying to help said patients in their distress. If this was meant to turn me on, it wasn't working! I didn't care if it had worked for him with dozens of others. How could I possibly feel safe around someone like that? It was a shame, too, because he was very good-looking, but he didn't bother to talk to me with any respect or to get to know me. He just assumed I would fall over backward and give him what he wanted. It reminded me eerily of my early relationships. *Not going there, ever again!*

Later, I was talking with a fellow medical student from my school who was also taking clinicals in New York. We were standing in one of the hospital foyers when the nearby elevator door opened, and Alan walked out on his way to somewhere else. He waved awkwardly at me when he saw me, giving me a sweet smile before walking away.

My friend saw him waving at me and said, "I know him. He's kind of a geeky guy."

"What do you mean?" I said, feeling annoyed at his comment. "I like him. I *like* nerds and geeks. At least they don't beat you up with their high opinion of themselves."

Several days later, I was doing medical rounds in the hospital with the orthopedic wolf pack, checking the patients' post-surgery progress. I peered into one doorway to see Alan bedside, dealing with a tearful patient. Although her surgery was successful, she was emotional with worry over her small children because she was stuck in the hospital. She and her husband had limited means and very little family support in the area.

I watched Alan quietly listen to her, not interrupting as I'd seen most doctors do. His face was concerned as if she was the only patient he had to care for that day. When she finally stopped crying, wiping tears from her face, she smiled at him, and I watched as he smiled back–a warm and genuine smile.

I sucked in a breath. *He sees her as a human being and not just as a surgical procedure in a medical chart!* Although he had not solved her family situation, by acknowledging what she was feeling, she felt comforted by his empathy and the giving of his time. I stood watching Alan, thinking, *the world lost a great psychiatrist when Dr. Oster went into orthopedics, but gained a great surgeon.* I witnessed Alan just being himself—a sweet, humble, kind person. I felt a twinge in my heart, a sparkle almost at those admirable traits, and something started to shift inside me regarding how I felt about him.

Until that moment, I wasn't sure if I was completely interested in him, even though I knew he liked me. Suddenly, I realized I did want to get to know him better. Geek or not, he was on my radar.

Over the ensuing days, whenever I got close to him, I was keenly aware of Alan's 6' 3" height to my 5' 3". While he towered over me and was physically massive compared to my small, slight frame, I was surprised by how safe

I felt around him. As a bisexual woman, I wondered about my attraction to him. Was it strange that after so many years of being with women, I now wanted to be with *him*? At least, I was considering being with him. I wasn't entirely sure yet.

As my orthopedic rotation continued, I got to know Alan better each day. During one deeper conversation we were having, he admitted that he had taken a full year off from his medical residency two years previously. His son's medical diagnosis had required significant interventions, and Alan took care of his son by himself.

I was floored. I had never heard of anyone taking a year off from a residency program, much less being able to successfully finish residency upon returning. It was a monumentally difficult thing to do. Alan had made a choice that could likely have ended his career as a doctor to help his son. His act of unselfish love moved me, and I couldn't let it go.

Trying to puzzle out my attraction to him, I realized I was falling in love... with Alan's soul, who he was as a human being. In my awe, I knew it wouldn't have mattered if he had been a man or a woman. I would have still loved the soul that lived *inside* his physical body. His gender was irrelevant to my love for him.

I thought Alan could be the one I wanted, but I still needed some advice.

Alan, although living separately from his wife, was still legally married. This was not the main issue for me. The biggest concern was that he was fifteen years younger than me! I was forty-four years old, and Alan was twenty-eight. After my shift that evening, I called my eldest daughter.

"Danni, I'm thinking of seeing someone. He's nice, but... he's fifteen years younger than me, which means he's only four years older than you. How do you feel about that?" I asked, worried about her reaction.

"Well, Mom, if you like him and he likes you, I don't see what the problem is," she said.

Wow, green light. I wasn't expecting that.

I ran into Alan in the hospital a couple of weeks after I finished my orthopedics rotation, and I decided to make the first move.

"Hey, Alan, we should go out for sushi one of these nights," I said casually.

He looked at me for a moment. "Sure, I'd like that, but I need to get back to you after I check my schedule," he said. I gave him my phone number, but he lost it somewhere later that day. Apparently, he wound up asking several of my fellow medical students, who were doing clinicals at the hospital, if they had my number.

As I learned *much* later, Alan was also seeking out dating advice. Alan told Paul Nero, one of the wolf pack, that he was planning to go out with me. A big grin came over Paul's face.

"Good," Paul said. "Do it for practice, Alan. Trust me, she's dirty. I can tell."

Alan was finally able to obtain my number, and two weeks later, he walked through my apartment door, dripping rain. Immediately, he kissed me. This was our first date.

It's been a long time coming, I thought, too thrilled to be too surprised. He was a busy third-year orthopedic surgery resident with little to no personal life, practically living at the hospital because he spent so much time there. As he held me, I loved that Alan was built like a grizzly. He was stocky, with enough fur on his body to keep a woman warm through a freezing winter. I liked to think of Alan as a bear walking on his back legs, especially as he had an adorable, shambling gait in which he dragged his feet, ruining his shoes. That night, Alan shuffled in the rain from the subway station to meet me at my apartment, four blocks away.

Noticing his hair was dripping onto his jacket, I asked him, "Do you need a blow dryer?"

He looked startled at my words but gave me a big smile, then paused, looking at me expectantly. Apparently, he had paid too much attention to Paul Nero's words.

I asked him again, "Umm, Alan... do you need a towel or a blow dryer?"

His look turned to confusion, then disappointment, before he shook his head and said, "No, I'm fine."

"Okay," I said, pulling my raincoat on. "Should we go to the restaurant now? Are you hungry?"

"Sure," he said, suddenly smiling again. "Let's go!"

He told me *much* later that he had thought I had asked him if he wanted something significantly different than a blow dryer, which goes to show you where his brain was. *What a dork.*

We went out to a little hole-in-the-wall Vietnamese restaurant in Brooklyn for pho—Vietnamese soup—and spent the meal talking about our lives and getting to know one another much more deeply. After dinner, Alan and I returned to my apartment to continue talking and spending time with each other. Against my better judgment, we wound up making out on the couch for a long while and then making love in bed. I found him too irresistible. Cuddling in bed after, I thought sleepily, *well, this relationship will probably go nowhere. I slept with him too soon! It's probably going to be just a casual sex thing.*

Nevertheless, I was enjoying the feeling of being wrapped in his arms, next to his large, hairy body, warm and cozy. I only rose from under the sheets to get something to drink from the kitchen. I was still chatting with him when he suddenly interrupted me.

"Jade, I love you." For all the world, he looked like a serious little boy.

I caught my breath. He sounded as if he was telling the truth. *Should I believe him?* I hesitated, but then my heart just cracked wide open and melted before I could stop it.

"Oh, Alan, I love you, too!"

A few days later, I was riding in a car in lovely New York City traffic with two friends of mine. Jason and Nahla were a striking, attractive couple and medical students like me. Jason was a tall, handsome man from Boston, like Alan. Nahla was Persian and gorgeous, with blond streaks in her long, dark hair. We were headed to a dinner meet & greet associated with the hospital.

"Dr. Oster told me he loved me after our first date," I admitted.

"What? Are you kidding me?" Jason laughed. "He's not serious! Don't believe him, Jade. That's what a lot of Boston guys say."

"Do you believe him, Jade?" Nahla asked. "It's kind of too soon to say that, isn't it?"

"Yes, it's way too early, but he seems to mean it," I said. "I guess time will tell."

"Just take it slow, and don't get your hopes up, Jade," Nahla said, her face serious.

Alan also shared our night. He told Paul that our date night included a rubber glove and an electric toothbrush. Paul could not contain his delight!

"I bet you brushed your teeth with it afterward! I know you did," Paul said gleefully. "I told you she was dirty. Trust me, I know. I'm going to tell everyone you had sex eight times. You'll be a legend!"

CHAPTER 16:

All the Love in the World

Once upon a time, there was a boy who loved a girl, and her laughter was a question he wanted to spend his whole life answering."
—Nicole Krauss

The next time Alan ran into Dr. Cho, Frank looked at him and cried, "You da man! Eight times, Alan!" Rumors spread quickly at the hospital.

As Alan and I first started to see each other regularly, I idly wondered if things would be different now that I was in a regular, sexual relationship with a man instead of a woman after so many years. The answer to my question was, *yes, different, and then some!* Alan, I discovered, was 1000% heterosexual, especially when you considered his sex drive and his fascination with my female body parts.

"It's not made of cast iron, Alan. Don't wear it out!" I teasingly reminded him.

I hadn't ever had this much sex in my life! Especially compared to Josh, the sexual desert. *So, this is what it's like to be in a relationship with a man fifteen years younger than me? Bring it on!*

It was a little overwhelming at first, but I soon got up to speed. *Thank you, God.* It seemed there would be a lot of touching in this relationship, and for the first time in my life, I would never be starving for affection. *I should probably marry him if he asks me,* I thought. *It doesn't take much to turn him on; every time I turn around, there's a stiffy!*

Alan was also a great cuddler. He loved to hold me in his arms, and I would caress his baby-soft skin as we talked for hours. With this much safety and affection, I could finally breathe again! I nestled close to his side with my body enclosed in his bulky arms, wrapped in his warmth and affection. *I can't believe how good this feels! Why did I have to wait until I was forty-four years old to meet this man?*

As we continued to date, I was hesitant to reveal everything about my past to Alan. The fear of losing him if I told him the truth became extremely stressful for me. Finally, I realized it wasn't worth the anguish I was going through. I decided I needed to tell Alan *everything*, and if he chose not to see me anymore, well, then I would know where I stood with him and I could get on with my life. At least, I already knew he was trustworthy.

So, finally, on a day off together about two months into our relationship, Alan and I returned from a visit to our favorite bagel cafe in Queens. This was it. I told Alan about my colorful past. To my relief, he listened kindly and attentively to the whole thing and was very accepting and non-judgmental. He thought it was rolling-on-the-floor hilarious that I had slept with more women than he had! (A lot more. But then, who's counting?) He eyeballed me sideways and joked, "You know, Jade, you're still in a gay relationship." He turned to face me, giving me a big, cheesy grin. "I'm really a lesbian inside."

I just rolled my eyes and looked at him. *What the heck does that mean?* I thought. *I mean, really?* Then, I got it. The man was referring to himself as a horn dog, which I already knew. *Whatever!*

"That's right, Alan, and you're just my dildo substitute." It was nice to know that I was such a source of entertainment for him. Still, my relief was palpable. Alan loved me for me—*all* of me. I'd never had a relationship like that before. I didn't have to be afraid or walk on eggshells. I didn't have to hide from him. I didn't have to go anywhere else for affection, nor did I want to. Plus, I could talk with him for hours and did so whenever we had a chance.

Alan and I spent almost all our limited free time together. We were so in love! And there was no shortage of laughter between us. One day, he noticed that when we were walking down a street in Manhattan, and an attractive woman walked by, we *both* turned around to look at her. Alan started laughing, and he laughed even harder when I gave him an annoyed look. He thought it was hysterical because he used to get in trouble with past girlfriends when they caught him looking at pretty girls.

Several months after Alan and I started dating, I ran into Neil, one of my fellow medical students, in the hospital hallway. He had been trying to get me to go out with him for months, but I knew he only wanted a one-night stand. I wasn't about to waste my time. He stopped me as I was about to walk into a patient's room, a chart in my hand.

"Jade, I forgot to tell you." He smirked and said, "Dr. Oster asked me for your phone number a couple of months ago."

I remembered Alan telling me he'd had to ask around to get my number after he'd lost it. Of course, he knew that all the medical students had each other's cell phone numbers for patient coordination care or in case of a patient emergency.

"I'm afraid I couldn't give it to him because I lost your number, Jade." He grinned at me, satisfied that he had successfully blocked Dr. Oster from his desire. It was obvious that Neil was still angry that I wouldn't go out with him.

"Oh, that's alright, Neil," I said, my voice carefully neutral and my face deadpan. "Dr. Oster—*Alan*—is moving into my apartment tomorrow. I just gave him a set of my keys." Then, I turned and walked away, leaving Neil with his mouth hanging open.

Paul Nero was surprised and a little disappointed that Alan and I became a couple and moved in with each other so quickly. As a long-time married man, he had anticipated a future of happily spreading pornographic rumors about Alan's adventures in dating.

"You better tell me every time you use her toothbrush," he gleefully smirked. "How great is that?"

The next year, having finished my last year of clinical rotations, I graduated from medical school. Alan and I had a quiet celebration, and my girls were proud of me. The big question of my last two years of medical school was what branch of medicine I was interested in going into. I had experienced rotations in orthopedics, general practice medicine, pediatrics, surgery, obstetrics and gynecology, and more. I had narrowed my interests down to two branches of medicine: Infectious Diseases and Psychiatry. From my background in volunteer work with HIV/AIDS patients, I was sure I would apply for a residency in Infectious Diseases, but when I had my clinical in psychiatry, headed by an incredibly brilliant and charismatic doctor, I was inspired to go into that field of medicine instead.

I applied and was accepted into the psychiatry residency program at a hospital in Harlem, New York City. It was a poverty-stricken, inner-city area plagued by a host of social problems, and I was chafing at the bit like a racehorse eager to get out there and run. I wanted to make a difference! Set up in a specialty that I loved and was excited about, I felt a sense of relief at my accomplishment and a new sense of purpose. After four years of medical school, I now faced four more years as a medical resident. *Halfway to the finish line!*

After Alan's divorce, we visited his dad in Boston. *Whew! No red flags!* What a lovely man his father was, genuine and kind. *Now I know where Alan gets all his great traits.* On the drive back home to New York, Alan suddenly proposed to me at a gas station. He didn't have a ring to give me, and he didn't get down on one knee. It didn't matter one whit; I was out of my mind with happiness and accepted on the spot!

Alan and I married before a judge, with Alan's buddy, Sam, as his best man. The judge's secretary got pulled in to be the second witness. Afterward, we went to Wendy's and had lunch. No wedding dress or church ceremony. No rings for either of us. No time or money for a honeymoon. We wanted to marry each other, so we just did it!

And then, we went back to our busy lives as medical residents. I heard a quote by Ellen G. White, and it made me think. "True love is not a strong, fiery, impetuous passion. It is, on the contrary, an element calm and deep. It looks beyond mere externals, and is attracted by qualities alone. It is wise and discriminating, and its devotion is real and abiding."

It seemed like the world believed that love was either all fiery and impetuous passion or that it was calm and abiding but devoid of passion.

I can't believe it. I've hit the jackpot! I've got a man who can't keep his hands off me - and vice versa - and yet, I feel our element of calm and deep. I felt we could neglect the world's ideas of "externals" like big weddings and expensive rings because we loved each other well beyond those elements. And despite what the world said, our devotion to each other was real and abiding.

I admired my husband, proud of the human being that he was. He was the type of person who attracted good people and good friends into his life, and they enjoyed being with him as much as I did. They were supportive of him and genuinely worried about him. With awe, I saw that Alan knew how to strike that balance between loving someone and allowing them to be themselves around him. He didn't require his friends to be just like him or think the same way he did. He didn't need to be arrogant or act like a god, despite his brilliance. Instead, like his father, I witnessed how Alan provided an environment that helped other people blossom, grow, and make decisions that truly belonged to them. My husband was my inspiration for what a truly nurturing relationship could be. And a fun one.

"How do you like having a cougar for a wife, Alan?" I would ask, smiling at him.

"How do you like having a cougar hunter for a husband, Jade?" he would say, placing both hands behind his neck, intertwining his fingers, and leaning back in his chair to look at me with a self-satisfied smirk.

Yes, in Alan's arms, I felt I was where I truly belonged. I had healed enough to attract a good man into my life. My relationship with Alan felt more wholesome and fulfilling than any relationship I had ever had. I felt safe with him—not judged, just loved. I didn't need anyone in my life to be whole now, but I wanted to be with Alan for all eternity. I felt like we had all the love and laughter in the world.

We would need every ounce of that for the rollercoaster of life—the momentary terrors and the trials, the laughter and the exhilaration... and all the miracles to come.

CHAPTER 17:

Riding the Rollercoaster

Out of the night that covers me,
Black as the Pit from pole to pole,
I thank whatever gods may be
For my unconquerable soul…

…It matters not how strait the gate,
How charged with punishments the scroll,
I am the master of my fate:
I am the captain of my soul.
—Ernest Hemingway, Invictus

I didn't tell Alan about the incident at work—at least, not right away. I had to get my head on straight first; plus, he was in Kentucky, engaged in study during his Orthopedic Trauma fellowship, and lapping it up. This man was not afraid of life, or people, or the things that happened to people and their bodies when they experienced traumas like accidents, gunshot wounds, or other things that caused complicated fractures around bone joints. He loved the specialty work that most other orthopedic surgeons wouldn't touch.

Those cases lit Alan's fire. He had a special touch; he helped make people whole again, body and soul. It just made me love him more.

But I couldn't ask him to help me with what just happened, so when he called for our evening touch-in and my voice was raspy, I made a pitiful excuse of coming down with a cold. Still, I adored Alan far too much to keep something from him, so I finally had to come out with it.

"Umm, remember a couple of weeks ago when I told you about my patient who drew me a lovely picture?"

"Yeah, I think I remember. The black gentleman you enjoy. If I remember, you said he was facing more than his fair share of mental and societal plagues... and you wished you could do more for him inside this screwed-up system of psychiatry. Same guy who drew that artistic likeness of you?"

"Yeah," I mumbled. "That one."

"Uh oh. What happened, Jade? Is he okay?" he asked somberly, knowing it could be any one of several things that plagued the Harlem community and hospital—one of the roughest sections in the entire nation.

"Well, he's okay," I said lamely. "It's just that I was with him at the nurse's station, talking to him about his meds. I had to look up at him; you know, he's super tall and towers over me like the high-rise buildings in Manhattan! One moment, we were talking, and then suddenly, I was writhing on the linoleum floor, gasping for air."

"You what?" he demanded. "Was it those damned meds again?"

"No, Alan, my meds have been okay." He was referring to a couple of months prior when my meds had screwed with my brain signals, and I'd fallen. "No, something triggered him—we can't figure out what—and well, he punched me in the throat. I never saw it coming. Neither did anyone else."

"Oh my God!"

"I swear, it came out of nowhere!" I blurted, hurrying to make sure he knew I was okay. "Luckily, the staff came running to assist me and remove him. It was only a few moments before I could finally gasp a full breath."

There was silence for a moment as he fathomed my words. We were both doctors, if still a bit fledgling, and we both knew what could have happened had my patient punched me harder. My windpipe could have been crushed. He didn't say it, but we both knew it; I could have died.

Despite my injury, with a hoarse voice and bruises on my neck, I returned to work the next day, to everyone's surprise. As I did my rounds, however, I felt like Don Quixote, tilting at windmills and too idealistic for my own good. *Maybe I need someone to put me in a padded room. Perhaps I should be in the room next to the one my patient is in?*

Alan checked on me daily. His sense of humor and ability to make light of difficult situations helped me to look more on the bright side of life. I was often way too serious about most things. Alan made me laugh when all I wanted to do was cry, and I would wind up laughing and crying at the same time and wanting to spank him for confusing me.

Just let me be upset and angry and paranoid, okay? Why do you have to make me smile? How dare you make me happy!

"You're the man of my dreams, Alan," I said one weekend when we could be together.

"Oy vey, so what's not to like?" he said, preening.

"Excuse me, hold on to your ego, Mister," I said. "Let's not get out of control here. I don't mean to criticize you, but even though you're a doctor, you have the emotional level of a twelve-year-old. You watch too much *Beavis and Butthead*, and your feet stink."

"So, what are you criticizing me about? Those are my good points!"

When he went back to Kentucky, we continued to check in with each other daily, as usual. Talking and laughing made us miss each other less, but I knew he worried about me. I was worried about myself. It wasn't that I faced this level of violence all the time. In fact, that was the only major incident I dealt with at the psychiatric hospital during my residency. The problem was that I was not as well as I pretended to be to my associates and fellow residents, especially under the microscope of my superiors.

Although I was blissfully happy to be married to Alan, I had struggled with depression for much of my life. I had nothing to pin my depression on while I was in medical school, except perhaps the overwhelming workload of the classes and the exams. One of the doctors at the school prescribed me an antidepressant, and it helped a lot. I was able to accomplish my work without a black fog following me around. However, by the end of my first year of residency, I noticed that the medication no longer worked. I went to my supervisor and asked for a recommendation for someone who could help me solve my problem, without talking to Alan about it first. When I mentioned it to him later, Alan was upset.

"I wish you hadn't done that, Jade," he said, his face worried. "You're in a residency program. They don't care if you're having issues with your mental health. They will eat you up and spit you out. Psych residency programs have the *least* tolerance for their residents having mental health issues than any other residency programs."

As it turned out, Alan was right. To compound the problem, my psychiatrist and my psychopharmacologist didn't agree on what meds I should be on, so I was bounced back and forth on different meds and different dosages–all with variable side effects. My body was on a rollercoaster.

One fateful morning, I was standing in our apartment, talking with Alan, when I suddenly toppled over. My body slammed hard onto the wooden floor! It happened so fast that Alan couldn't catch me. My whole body went stiff, and I couldn't even bring my arms up in front of me to protect myself from the fall. Amazingly, I wasn't hurt when Alan helped me up, but this was just one horrific side effect of the psychiatric meds I'd been prescribed. The medical cocktail was a recipe for disaster.

As time and my studies progressed, I was learning firsthand how the mental health system was screwed up. There were too few beds, too many fakers reselling their meds, and too great a reliance on ineffective prescriptions for those who had genuine mental illnesses. I prayed for my patients, but instead of also praying for myself, I berated and chided myself in my head. *I knew I should have gone into Infectious Diseases! You can't fake that. You either have cholera, or you don't!*

In the meantime, Alan and I were living in two separate cities, which was expensive. We'd both lived alone for long periods, and we were both used to tremendous study and workloads and being radically busy. It wasn't that we couldn't live without each other. But now that we had found one another, we didn't like living apart.

Still, we needed my paycheck, so I toughed out my residency program as long as I could. The humiliation and stress of it was excruciating. A slow-moving trainwreck, I knew I was failing the program. It was horrible when they fired me—one of the most shameful and traumatizing events of my life, and it felt like the biggest failure I'd ever experienced.

Fortunately for us, when Alan started his fellowship, he began receiving a paycheck. Although I felt deeply ashamed of failing my residency, I was relieved to leave New York and move to Kentucky to be with my husband. Our separate living situations had been incredibly hard and lonely for both of us. It was good for our marriage to be living together again, but I carried that dark cloud of failure with me.

For a time in Kentucky, I went into what I called my Great Depression. I kept having dreams, or rather nightmares, that I was back in med school or my residency program, panicking and searching for something. It was always frantic, this search for some missing piece to the puzzle to fix my failure. Too demoralized to try again, I never did apply to another residency program, although I could have.

It took years, but eventually, I came out of the depression. In fact, I found a great light at the end of the tunnel! I chose to stay home and be a housewife to support Alan's busy schedule. I also became an entrepreneur and helped my husband start up his side gig, a residential and commercial real estate business.

It was Alan's dream to own rental property. I got excited about it, and it became *our dream*. I took classes online in real estate, got my real estate agent's license, and found houses for my husband to invest in. As an adult, I had developed a nose for money—I can almost smell it—and it started paying off. I advised Alan about which houses to buy and the price he should pay, and our business began to grow nicely.

I also took classes in property management, home inspection, construction, painting and drywall, plumbing, renovating old houses, wiring, and HVACs. I even began renovating houses and apartments, mostly painting, drywall, cabinets, and flooring. Although we hired plumbers, electricians, HVAC vendors, and other service people, now I could at least speak their language.

For example, I saved us tens of thousands of dollars by coming up with a solution to a plumbing problem that even the plumber hadn't thought of. He agreed it would work, and it did. Problem fixed! My confidence grew again, and so did much of my happiness.

Transformations

Almost four years after Alan and I married, a friend of ours gave birth, and we went to visit her and her brand-new baby daughter in the hospital. Holding that little baby made me yearn to have a child–with Alan!

Impossible, I thought. I watched him hold her, seeing that big man transformed into a pile of mush by a tiny newborn. Instead of holding that baby in the palm of his large hand, I watched him cradle her, and at that very moment, I knew I wanted to have children with him.

Maybe not so impossible.

I trusted Alan. He had proven himself to me since we had been married; I couldn't have wished for a kinder, gentler husband. Babies and animals loved him. Knowing that meant the world to me.

Later that evening, I cuddled next to Alan on the couch and wrapped my arms around his middle, hugging him to me as I would hug a pillow.

"Alan, you looked so happy holding Alicia today in the hospital."

"Yep," he admitted, "she is very, very cute, just a button." He looked at me shyly. I noticed the wistfulness in his voice as he added, "She almost makes me want to have more children... children with you, Jade." I stared at him.

"Alan, I want to have children with you, too."

"Are you sure?" His eyes lit up.

"Yes, Alan, I'm sure," I said, grinning. "We make a great team. We've been married for almost four years. I can't think of anyone I'd want to have children with more than you, my sweet husband."

"That would be great!" he said, and I witnessed one of the biggest smiles on his face I'd ever seen. "Me, too," he continued, "although we both know we'll probably face some challenges. Do you want to see what our options are?" I laughed and nodded enthusiastically.

Alan, at thirty-three years old, was still young enough to want more children, but it would likely be difficult for me, at forty-eight, to be able to carry a child. I'd not only had my tubes tied, but I was postmenopausal. We knew we were unlikely to succeed, but we made an appointment with an IVF (in vitro fertilization) specialist to see what our chances might be.

They said what we already knew. There were no guarantees. Did we want to risk it? IVF was very costly, and we were told that it might take more than one expensive procedure to successfully get me pregnant. It was a lot of money, time, and emotional risk just on the *chance* that we could have a child of our own.

We brainstormed with the specialists. Because the eggs in my ovaries were too old to have a solid chance of being viable, we were told to consider an anonymous donor egg from a woman much younger than me to increase our odds of success. Within weeks, we found a donor who sounded lovely, and she went through the procedure. Alan and I were lucky enough to get five viable embryos. I had to give myself daily hormone shots and pills to get my body ready, and then two of the embryos were implanted in my uterus. Unfortunately, we lost them. Alan and I were heartbroken at the loss. I sobbed to my daughter, Danni, on the phone about how upset we were.

"Don't cry, Mommy," Danni said. "I'll donate my eggs to you. You'll have babies with my eggs, I promise."

My daughter kept her word, and eight months later, we had four viable embryos from Danni, two of which were implanted in my womb. We waited, a little more guarded. Emotionally, it was something I'd never experienced. *Would it work this time? Was it even possible for my body to support life?* It felt like we were holding our breath.

In the ob-gyn office, we listened as the doctor searched around with the ultrasound wand. He grinned as he found a heartbeat. I looked at Alan, and his face crumpled. Tears of joy streamed down our faces. Then suddenly, the doctor said, "And... here is the other one."

The other one?

Alan and I stared at each other. I wanted to jump up and down in joy, but that would have been a little awkward for me in my hospital gown. Instead, I settled for a huge Alan bear hug and his tears mixed with mine.

Danni's gift gave us our first children together. Further tests revealed a set of fraternal twins, a boy and a girl. We were out of our minds with happiness! Danni flew in for my induced C-section, and as the biological mother, the hospital made an exception and allowed her to be present in the delivery room when our twins were born. After being discharged from the hospital, I loved taking care of my beautiful, little, precious babies, Lila and Harrison. I rarely let Alan change their diapers, teasing him, "You'll drop them. I'll take care of them. What do you know about babies? You're a man."

Obviously, I hogged our little tykes, but in my mind, it was "mommy and me" time. My whole world consisted of my babies. The oxytocin was working on overdrive! I was blissfully happy to stay at home to be a housewife and mother. After working long, chaotic hours at the hospital, Alan was happy to come home to a peaceful family waiting for him. It was a pleasure to watch him hold them on his chest and nuzzle them contentedly. And oh, how they adored their dad!

One night, I got up to feed two hungry babies, and after I put them back to bed, I marveled as I looked out the bedroom window at the moonlit Kentucky sky. From the time I was a little girl, I'd wanted to be a housewife and a mother. The world told me over and over that it wasn't possible, and I'd lived almost my entire life with that lie—that I couldn't be happy being at home. Now, I was so grateful, in sheer bliss. It might not be every woman's dream, but it had been mine since I could remember. And somehow, God was watching over me, even though I didn't deserve His care. We had two little ones to cherish! And I would love them and protect them with my life's breath.

CHAPTER 18:

Grace, Gratitude & Diamonds

"Let gratitude be the pillow upon which you kneel to say your nightly prayer. And let faith be the bridge you build to overcome evil and welcome good."
—Maya Angelou

A year later, Alan and I and the fertility team tried IVF again with the last two embryos from Danni. It worked again, and all three of us were euphoric when we got pregnant with another baby. This pregnancy was filled with worry because I bled through much of the early months. We were worried that I was going to miscarry, and my life was at risk.

What a miracle when we gave birth to a beautiful baby girl who we named Alyssa! The twins were fascinated with her, this infant-sized version of my wee toddlers. They quickly grew to love and adore her. (Of course, the adoration would stop when she grew old enough to take their toys.)

Two months after her birth, I took my newborn daughter, held safe in my arms, for a swim with me in a wading pool warmed by the hot August sun. Once again, we were filled with God's grace, though I didn't know why–but that didn't keep me from being incredibly grateful. As I waded in the warm water, watching my tiny one's expressions at the experience, I marveled.

At a flash of memory, I gasped. Almost twenty-five years prior, when I was a member of the Church of Jesus Christ of Latter-day Saints, a clergy member, the patriarch of our branch, had given me a special "patriarchal blessing." In it, he told me that I would bring more children into this world. As much as I enjoyed feeling the Spirit of the prayer, I thought this gentleman was, quite possibly, off his rocker! I was with Josh, and I'd already had my tubes tied from my previous marriage. At the time, his words seemed impossible.

Now, as I held this precious little one in my arms, with my twins safely with my husband, I realized I had waited for a very long time for those promises to be made manifest in my life. I now had some idea of what Sarah and Abraham (Genesis 18:13-14) had gone through as they waited years for the promised blessings. Like Sarah, God gave me a child in my old age—and more than just one child! Although I would not have a good night's sleep for six years straight, I didn't regret any of it and loved caring for my beautiful babies. I loved being a mother, happy and secure with a husband who loved me and our family.

Bobbing gently in the water, I thought about how I didn't consider myself worthy of God's care or attention, yet it was evident that God's love never failed. *Why would He gift me with such sweetness? How could God bless me after I had left Him and wandered so far from His side?* Deep in my heart, I felt so ashamed that I had been rebellious and had gone off the rails to wander alone on strange roads.

I've strayed too far from Him. How can I go back? How do I get back to Him? Where do I go? I had so many questions, but even though I was lost, I was not lost to Him. I was discovering throughout all of this that He was mindful of me. I was important to Him. For whatever reason, my happiness mattered to Him.

At that moment, I vowed to live a better life, not just for my own sake but for the sake of my beautiful, growing family.

A year and a half after the birth of our third child, we used the frozen embryos we had left from our anonymous donor, and I got pregnant once more. I gave birth to another lovely, sweet daughter, Evie, for a total of four children in a little over three years.

Alan and I considered ourselves incredibly, gloriously blessed to have been gifted by God with four beautiful babies, especially because of my age of fifty years plus, when so many younger women were not able to have a child, even after doing IVF repeatedly. This was truly a miracle from God.

When my children were still in baby carriers and car seats, I would pile them in the car and take them with me to do drive-bys to scope out houses I was interested in perhaps buying. Together, we would check out the neighborhood, my minivan full of happy chatter, bottles, binkies, and sippy cups. If it wasn't a good neighborhood or there was something funky about the neighbors, we wouldn't buy the house. Alan continued to work all day as a doctor.

I loved it when our accountant told us our mom-and-pop business was doing extraordinarily well. We never bought a money pit nor had to cut our losses on any piece of real estate. It seemed God was blessing that, too, and I loved being able to significantly contribute to my family's well-being, emotionally, physically, and financially. With great pleasure, we paid off both of our medical school loans.

While my husband and I had our share of problems and difficulties, like any married couple, we grew together and found peace with each other. We continued to polish each other's rough edges and bring out the gold hidden behind the dross.

How could a marriage like ours work? I didn't know. It was a mystery to me. You could just as well ask me why the wildebeest migrate on the Serengeti Plain in Africa. I didn't know the answer to that question, either. To some people, the differences in our age and life experiences made us an odd couple, but we fit into each other like puzzle pieces meant to be connected, side by side. We continued to be true partners in our journey together, holding hands and facing our future, come what may.

I hadn't realized, until I met Alan, that God had heard my prayers all those years ago when I was married to Josh. God not only answered my prayers, but he sent the perfect man for me. Our relationship, though loving and respectful, continued to be full of bawdy humor and irreverence to convention. We bantered back and forth constantly with one-liners, like playing a game of ping pong.

Thankfully for me, my husband was a very low-maintenance partner. I once joked that if I gave him enough food and sex, I could ignore him for days and he'd be perfectly okay with it. That gave me more time to watch YouTube.

After having cuddle time with Alan, I would often say to him, "Don't expect me to talk to you again unless I'm horny. Probably in two to three days, unless it's earlier. You know I don't even like you. I just keep you around for sex. Thank you, drive-thru."

Alan would smirk and say, "Yep, that's all I'm good for. Just to service you."

Good boy! It's nice that he knows his place. Talk dirty to me, baby!

In case you think Alan was simply funny and a complete saint, I have to set the record straight. Except when I was pregnant, Alan and I occasionally drank alcohol. One Thanksgiving Eve, after the kids were put to bed, we decided to have some pre-holiday drinks. He was off for a couple of days for the holiday weekend, barring any emergencies. We made some White Russians, topped off by Kahlua and cream drinks. I had two drinks and stopped. Alan kept drinking and got very drunk.

In all the years that Alan and I had been together, I had seen him drunk probably four times, and two of those times were in the first year we were together. He rarely imbibed in alcohol. That evening, he made up for the prior ten years of not drinking, and he became what I would call "sloppy drunk." To my chagrin, he didn't want to go to sleep. He wanted to stay up all night and raise hell. I was infuriated because I had to get up at 4:30 a.m. to put the turkey in the oven and make all the other side dishes, but here I was babysitting his sorry, drunk butt.

After a series of drunken shenanigans, I finally got Alan into the shower and then into bed.

Alan decided he was feeling horny. "I want some, Bebe!"

"No, go to sleep. I have to get up in a few hours to cook."

"But I *want* some!"

"Shhh! Be quiet!"

"*I want some!*"

"Shhh! Shut up! Okay, you can have it, but it will cost you two thousand dollars"

Alan suddenly looked like he had sobered up a bit. There's nothing like having an expensive bill to sober my cheap husband up. He looked like he was thinking hard.

"Why so mus-ssh?" he said, garbling his words, taking me seriously.

"Because I am pissed," I said. "Let's just call it a tax for pissing me off."

Alan and I were made for each other. I giggled afterward and went to sleep. But you can bet I held him to that tax the next morning, even though I put it in our family's emergency fund! We eventually just stopped drinking. He, because he rarely had days off, and I, because I acted just as idiotic as Alan if I drank too much. I didn't need that anymore. I wanted to be responsible for the safety of my young kids.

After our tenth anniversary, Alan asked if I wanted a wedding ring set. As poor medical residents, we'd never exchanged rings when we married. I thought about it and then bought a couple of fake wedding ring sets I liked from Walmart, online. They looked real! I got the same wedding ring set in two sizes, my normal ring size and the next larger size for when my fingers swelled. Together, both ring sets cost me around forty-five dollars.

I was ecstatically happy. I showed them to Alan when they came in the mail.

"Jade, those rings are pretty, but I meant that I'll buy you *real* diamonds. You can pick out exactly what you want."

"Thank you, Alan. I love you, too, but I like these rings. I'm happy with them. I don't need real diamonds."

I was happy with my fake diamonds and wore my rings most places, until one day, I was shopping in the Goodwill (one of my favorite stores, as old habits die hard) and noticed a guy staring at my wedding ring with a keen, fixed interest. The fake diamond on my wedding ring was larger than it had seemed in the picture when I bought it, and it looked real and very expensive. I thought to myself, *great, I'm going to get beaten and robbed for a twenty-two-dollar, fake diamond ring!* I loved cheap jewelry and had no need to buy real gold or diamonds, so it sucked when I couldn't even wear my fake stuff!

When I got home, Alan could tell I wasn't in a great mood.

"What happened?" he asked, and I told him about the incident.

"Did I tell you?" he deadpanned. "I just got robbed by six dwarfs. Not Happy."

CHAPTER 19:

Safety in the Storm

"I'm selfish, impatient and a little insecure. I make mistakes. I am out of control and at times hard to handle. But if you can't handle me at my worst, Then you sure as hell don't deserve me at my best."
—**Marilyn Monroe**

The news was shattering. It was September 2020, and the world was in quarantine due to the pandemic. Mom was in Hawaii and not doing well, but it was nearly impossible, not wise, and even frightening to fly. My family told me not to bother coming because we weren't allowed to see her in the hospital. It was crushing.

She declined quickly and was gone. They were only allowed to hold a tiny funeral. Less than a handful gathered when normally there would have been hundreds of us. Under different circumstances, I would have been there in a heartbeat. But we couldn't.

Outside our purposely peaceful little family in Kentucky, it seemed like the world was full of panic and strife. People were dying from this strange virus, and the whole world seemed to be tilting.

Up until then, I tried not to let it bother me. I knew situations and circumstances in the world would come and go. So many already had. My stint in medicine and weathering the rises and falls in real estate were proof of that. Alan had also weathered many local and world tragedies. His 9-11 experience stayed with me all those years after he shared it with me. As difficult as the medical crisis was, we knew this, too, would pass.

In the meantime, I copied a design for cloth face masks that I saw on the news, double-layered with a pocket to insert an additional paper surgical facemask for extra protection. I sewed about a hundred of them to keep my family safe. I wanted to ensure that everyone in my family always had access to a clean face mask, especially since the hospitals and stores were running out of their supplies. We all wore them religiously to keep each other safe. I'd seen microbes under microscopes. I'd seen the refrigerated trucks outside our friends' apartments in New York. We were playing it safe.

The cloth face masks, unlike the disposable paper ones, could be easily washed and reused. Alan was working at Ground Zero for the virus, in the hospitals with sick patients. We were both terrified that he might catch the virus or bring the virus home to our family. As soon as he walked in the door from work each day, he took off his clothes and facemask, put them straight into the washing machine, and showered before ever hugging our children and me.

But inside our little haven, our children, now ages ten (times two), nine, and seven years old, were growing like the beautiful flowers in my garden and most often looked to me for guidance. They were schooling from home, on the computer, as were their classmates, and despite the disruption, I sought to make life as normal as possible.

Yet, at the news of my mom's passing, I felt an absence of feeling under my skin, as if I were frozen in ice.

Strangely, in the hours and days that followed, as I began to thaw, I realized I had held onto my feelings of anger over the traumatic experiences of my life. Yet a lot of the anger I'd held for so long died when my mom died. I had suspected for years that my mom, too, had been sexually abused as a child and had suffered in silence her whole life. As I looked back on my childhood, it seemed that my dad's behavior toward me was normalized and familiar to her. I grieved for her unspoken pain. As I thawed, I became raw because now it was time to mourn the amazing woman that she was. I became bereft.

I was sleepwalking through my days, lost and adrift, crying and grieving, especially at the realization that I had blamed my mom for my traumatic experiences with my dad. The truth was, he had passed before I'd had time to confront him and resolve my unfinished issues with him. Because of his elevated sense of entitlement, he was oblivious to the damage he had done to both my mother and me.

I had learned the lesson way too young that "men do what they want." And he did. There was far too much that I had left unsaid to him. I had shoved all my feelings of rage and helplessness at my dad down deep in my gut for decades. The harsh truth was that because I couldn't spew it onto him, I had projected it onto my mom, sometimes being cold and callous to her. As I processed my feelings, I didn't have the heart to be angry with her anymore.

Now, the scalding truth hit home: I missed her, but it was too late. There was also far too much that I had left unsaid with her. What made me cry was knowing I couldn't even tell her how sorry I was for my anger and resentment of her choices, for choosing my father over protecting me. I knew she had often felt my anger, even though I had never stated it openly to her. She had suffered in silence at my treatment of her just as she had suffered in silence at my dad's treatment of her.

To know I had added insult to injury wounded me the deepest. How could I have acted that way toward someone I loved so deeply, even so unconsciously? *Could I be doing that to others that I love?* Another thought hit me that made my blood run cold. *Could I be doing that to God?*

The way I saw my life suddenly shifted monumentally. Something certainly shifted in the way I *wanted* to live my life, but what was it?

Now, I felt a clock ticking inside of me—but it was a different sort of clock this time. I could feel it in my heartbeat. It wasn't regarding fear for my children. They were all as safe as possible in the current circumstances. No, this had to do with my life on earth and my soul.

One evening, I looked out the window at the glorious colors and falling leaves without seeing a thing. *I haven't made my relationship right with God, and I don't want to die this way!* With all my heart, I wanted to get square with God. The clock was ticking louder and louder for me, as it does for every soul.

I knew that clock would stop one day.

On the news, nurses told of some patients who were dying from the virus. When some patients were told they had the pandemic virus, they angrily shook their fists at the doctors and nurses and called them liars, saying there was no virus. The tragedy, infighting, shortsightedness, and uselessness of what humanity was experiencing during the pandemic was too awful for words.

I don't want to die like that, I thought. *I don't want to die angry.* In so many ways, God had been trying to tell me the truth my whole life. The truth that Jesus Christ was The Good Shepherd and if I followed Him, He would lead my soul to safety (Psalm 23). *I don't want to fight with God until my dying breath! I don't want to fight with Him at all anymore. So, what do I do now?*

Suddenly, with my mother gone, there were so many questions I had no answers to. Was I living the life I wanted to live? Or was I mindlessly following the road I was already traveling on? Did I have to continue the rebel path I had chosen so many years ago? If the path I was on had no purpose or meaning for me *now*, could I choose to travel a different road?

I didn't know, and I flailed around, searching for answers. Frankly, I was tired of living in a spiritual and emotional wasteland, except for my loving family. Also, I missed that deep feeling of love I had felt from the Spirit when I attended church, and especially the temple, all those years ago. I remembered the miracle I had experienced once when I tried to commit suicide so long ago, and I could still feel the love my Heavenly Father had surrounded me with, enclosing me within it. He had made a promise to me. *No matter what happens to you in this life, you're going to be okay.*

I was done with my exile. I knew from my life experiences that I couldn't trust the world, but I knew I could trust Alan, and I knew I could trust God. It was time to go Home.

But, I wondered, *could I go home?* With over thirty years of wandering on strange roads, I had strayed very far away from my God. Did my Heavenly Father still love me? Would I, with all my sins, be welcomed back home? Could I be forgiven if I gave up all my sins to know Him?

In the Bible, the Pharisees often criticized Jesus for eating with sinners, tax collectors, and people of low status. These people were often invisible to the elite religious leaders of His day but not to Jesus. He welcomed all who came to Him.

Maybe I'm not invisible to Him, too.

As another few weeks passed in a gloom and 2020 dragged on, I watched the news and realized I had never before seen trouble of this magnitude in the world. So many natural disasters. So many people dying from the pandemic. And it was just getting started. Who knew where it would end? There was so much hatred and fighting over how to deal with the pandemic. People were splitting off into tribes, isolating themselves, and not working together. Ugliness, division, conspiracy theories, and name-calling were rampant, on a level I had never seen before. So much evidence of man's inhumanity to man.

Then I thought, *with all this ugliness, who can I trust to have my back?*

I remembered that most of my fellow worshipers in the Church of Jesus Christ of Latter-day Saints were at least *trying* to live a good life and be good people, unlike many people I saw on the news and in grocery stores, not even trying to be kind to their fellow man. I concluded that there still had to be many good people in the world. I had met too many wonderful, generous people from all walks of life not to know that. But out of all the groups of people I'd met, the only group I felt I could *trust* were members of the Church of Jesus Christ of Latter-day Saints.

Yes, I knew they were imperfect people. I knew there were tares among the wheat. It was their *struggle* to be good, to be kind, and to grow to be more like the Savior, Jesus Christ, that set them apart for me. They were that shining city on a hill, surrounded by the darkness, strife, and chaos of the Wilderness. Furthermore, even if the Church members were imperfect, as all humans are, I knew, from the depths of my soul, that my Heavenly Father and Jesus Christ were perfect and held a perfect love for me, always.

I felt a sudden warmth. The love He surrounded me with was like a shield protecting me from the coldness of the world. Because I had experienced for myself the kindness and tender mercies of my Heavenly Father, I realized, with a gasp, just how much I missed Him and longed for Him. My soul hungered. *Yes*, it was time to come Home.

I turned away from the window and made a decision. It was a crazy decision. It was probably crazier than anything I had ever done in my entire *tan loca* life!

On a chilly October day, about a month after my mom's death, I contacted the missionaries through the Church of Jesus Christ of Latter-day Saints website and requested missionary visits. They sent out two young men to visit. Alan was at work, but he was so supportive of my needs. "Whatever you need to do, Bebe." He always supported me in making my own decisions. My kids were home and curious about these two young men in their masks, as all visitors had to wear them when indoors during this time.

Talking to them felt great. *Why didn't I do this years ago?* As I looked at their kind eyes, I knew the answer was because I had wandered too far for too long.

After their visit, I found the closest ward church online. I got the kids dressed, and even Alan joined us for the next sacrament meeting, all of us wearing our masks. I didn't get struck by lightning as we walked through the door!

I felt shy, but covered my shyness by being outgoing and smiling, pushing down my trepidation of not fitting in. Walking into the chapel, I noticed other people were friendly and welcoming, and I at least knew the missionaries who were there. They were surprised and thrilled to see us.

Quaking inside, I kept it together for the sake of my kids, even though, emotionally, I was drowning. Since Mom died, I hadn't been able to sleep, and I couldn't eat. It felt as if there was a black rock in my stomach, weighing me down and making me nauseous. As we entered a pew and sat down together, I prayed. *I surrender, Father. Please help me!*

As I sat there, the old worries filled my mind. *Would God be mindful of me in my grief?* This was the turning point, the perfect storm, overpowering anything I had experienced in my life before. I decided to attend church every Sunday, and I would continue to see the missionaries. I never faltered.

Alan was incredibly supportive. He did not have the same spiritual interest as I did, but he quickly saw how this would be good for our children and our family. Every Sunday that he didn't have to go to work, he helped me get the kids up and dressed, and attended church with us. It became part of our family time together.

Talking to the missionaries, I asked what steps I needed to take to regain my membership. I longed to go and worship my Heavenly Father in our temple, the House of the Lord. I prayed to Him daily now for peace and comfort. When the missionaries responded that I needed to get baptized, I felt so much relief and comfort. I asked them a million questions and focused hard on what I needed to learn and do. As I attended the weekly meetings at church, I felt more and more accepted and was able to relax because the other people were so warm and kind to my family and me.

The Spirit was very strong around me when the missionaries were present, and when I was alone. One day, I was alone in the kitchen, cleaning something, when suddenly, an overpowering feeling of love dropped down on me like a veil or a scarf, so much so that it startled me, stopping me in the middle of my task and making me catch my breath. I was enveloped by the Spirit, with a loving certainty that Father was pleased with me and the steps I was taking to return to Him, to get back on the covenant path. Instead of literally being afraid of lightning striking me, I now felt a sense of peace and love as I sat in the chapel on Sundays with my family, feeling closer to my Father and Jesus Christ than I'd felt in decades.

I was striving to be reconciled with my Father, and although it was difficult and emotional at times, I was determined to press on.

CHAPTER 20:

The Road Home

"The greatest glory in living lies not in never falling, but in rising every time we fall."
—**Nelson Mandela**

While studying with the missionaries, I asked what the process was for being admitted back into the church after being excommunicated. They told me I needed to complete my lessons with them first. Then, I could request an interview with the Stake President and two other priesthood holders who would decide whether I could be rebaptized. These men were church members who held higher offices in the church.

During the interview, I would have to confess my sins. If they agreed that I could be rebaptized, that could happen fairly quickly. After baptism, I would be on probation for a year, after which I could apply to get my endowments restored. I would then be allowed my dream—to go to the temple to worship God. The Latter-day Saints members go to temples to perform sacred ordinances, such as baptisms, endowments, and sealings, to unite all of God's children, both the living and the dead, into eternal families.

On the day of my interview with the Stake President, I noticed President Kenning had a tremendous, gentle spirit. Just being around his energy was comforting. Two of his counselors, men who held the priesthood, would also sit in on the interview with me.

As I walked into the room, I remembered my reaction when the missionaries had first told me I would have to confess my sins. *Yeah, yeah, confess your sins. I got it,* I thought.

I must have blown past that requirement in my mind, not really paying attention at the time. But now, I was in a conference room facing three strangers who were handing me a shovel to dig up my past. *What? Who wants to dig up that moldy, stinking corpse? Not me!*

"What sins would you like to confess, Jade?" President Kenning asked, sounding kind but firm. I was sitting at one end of a very long table; the three men were all sitting at the other end. Feeling nervous, I noticed a weird churning in my stomach and the sensation of goosebumps running up my arms from my wrists to my shoulders. My discomfort wasn't from the air-conditioner. Everyone was wearing a face mask because we were in the middle of a pandemic, and I couldn't read the expressions on their faces to gauge their reaction to me. *I'm flying blind,* I thought, panicked. *I hope I don't crash and burn.*

"It has to be a full confession of all your sins since you left the church," explained President Kenning.

Oh, crap, I thought, coughing and clearing my suddenly dry throat. *This isn't going to be good. A lot of sinning can be done in thirty years!* Puzzled, I was not sure where to start. *Do they want an item-by-item list, or can I put my sins into broad categories? Oh, boy... this could be a long interview. We could be here all week!*

It had been a long time since I had lived my wild life, my purple past, and most of it, I didn't want to remember! I was ashamed and traumatized by many of my memories, which were saturated and heavy with my tears and regrets.

For some time now, almost twenty years, I had been in a monogamous relationship with my husband, Alan. We had been married for eighteen of those years. In addition to his two children and my two children, we had four more children together for a total of eight kids. At sixty years old, I was settled into a conventional, peaceful life and was hopefully wiser than I had been in my younger, stupid years.

Is this really necessary?

I felt scared and discouraged. Freezing, I pulled my jacket around me like a blanket, trying to find some warmth. My fear of their reaction to what I had to confess was almost more than I could stand! I knew that in confessing my sins, I would feel shamed and humiliated. No one knew my past in its entirety except for my husband, Alan, who was not a member of the church. He thought some parts of my past were incredibly funny, but I didn't think President Kenning or his counselors would find any of it amusing. I was afraid that I would shock them and that their reaction would increase my feelings of deep humiliation.

The silence was deafening. President Kenning finally covered his mouth with his hand and coughed as he looked at me. It was time.

I'll start off small, I decided.

"Umm... I haven't followed the Word of Wisdom. I've drunk alcohol, coffee, tea, and used tobacco. I did some drugs after I left the church. It wasn't a lot. And it wasn't anything serious like heroin or cocaine." Full stop.

Take a breath, Jade.

"I committed adultery thirty years ago when I was married to my husband, Josh." I paused, dreading what came next.

President Kenning and his counselors waited quietly, listening.

Continuing to talk, expanding on my sins for quite some time, I told them of all the pain I felt from what other people had done to me, and I told them of all the pain I felt from what I had done to other people.

President Kenning nodded, acknowledging my sorrow, and gently said, "It matters how you treat people; it really matters."

The three men sat in the room, quietly listening to me as I continued to confess my sins. It had been a long time since my sins had seen the light of day, and I was wishing boulders would fall on me and hide me from their gaze.

I was so mortified that I briefly considered lying, but I knew God knew all my sins, and I couldn't hide from Him. Like the prodigal daughter, for the very first time in my travels, my desire to come home was stronger than any humiliation or shame I felt, and I knew I couldn't come home unless I told the truth.

"Let me think; it was all a long time ago. I'm trying to remember." I slowed down, trying to delay speaking the words of what I didn't want to reveal. "I've also had relationships with women—sexual relationships with women." This statement came out in a loud, defiant tone due to my chagrin. "I worked as a dancer for a while in a strip club," I blurted and stopped.

My God, I thought, suddenly panicking, *why do I have to confess these things? I committed these sins in my twenties and thirties! I'm sixty-one years old now!*

I shut my mouth, unwilling to go any further.

"Anything else, Jade?" President Kenning said, trying to encourage me. I looked at him, trying to guess his reaction to my words.

Yep, he knows what's coming next, I thought. *He's either figured it out, or Father told him.*

Anger rose up in me—really... deep... down... anger, on top of the fear and shame filling every cell in my body. I was shaking with it now. *I do not want to do this, but it's the only way home.* I was struck by a thought. *How can I confess my sins to people who may or may not have ever even got a parking ticket?* I wasn't exaggerating; thirty years ago, I knew a Sister Carol who had never got a ticket in her life!

Okay, Heavenly Father, here it comes. "I also did some prostitution." There, it was out—my worst shame.

Another silence filled the room, and President Kenning seemed to know I was done. I was also spent. "Do you repent from all these sins, Jade?" he said kindly.

"Yes, I do," I said. I meant it.

"You know that if you commit these sins again, Jade, you will forfeit your membership in the church, and you may not get it back. Do you understand that?" he said.

"Yes, I do," I said. I meant that, too.

"Is there anything you would like to add, Jade?" he said.

"Yes, President Kenning, I do have something else I'd like to say." I paused again, but this time, it was a different kind of pause. My voice was stronger as I continued. "I don't know why I've had the experiences I've had in my life to take with me into the Eternities, but I know that my Heavenly Father has a plan for my life. I know that things happen in my life on His timeline and for His purposes. And I know that my Heavenly Father loves me," I said firmly. "This I know for a fact, right down to my bones."

He nodded. "Thank you, Jade. We'll be back in a short while."

The men rose from their chairs and left the room to confer and decide my fate. I sat alone and prayed to my Father. As I reached out to Him with my whole soul, I felt that peaceful, beautiful voice that had once spoken to me and saved my life so long ago in a bathroom at the top of a house.

"It is good."

Tearful and exhausted, I knew He had answered me, and I wept.

About fifteen minutes later, the men came back into the room. Immediately, President Kenning's face was softer, and I noticed smile lines around his eyes. He said, "We've decided that you can be rebaptized." My heart leaped for joy, even as he added, "But understand that you will not be able to go to the temple for a year until you get your endowments back. Your endowments are your church blessings. To get your endowments back and become a temple-attending member of the church again, you will have to get approval from the First Presidency of the Church in Salt Lake City."

My eyes went wide. *All the way to the First Presidency? The prophet and his two counselors?*

"With you, we will submit your request for reinstatement to them one year after you've been baptized. We will detail your progress on the covenant path by following the commandments as laid out in the holy scriptures, your level of activity in the church, your tithe-paying, and whether you are following the Word of Wisdom."

I nodded. *Not a problem!*

Relieved to be done with the interview, I felt ecstatic. Joy coursed through my body, but as I made my way outside and climbed into my car, I was physically and emotionally exhausted. All I could do was utter a silent prayer, thanking my Father for His love and mercy and my Redeemer, Jesus Christ, for His great sacrifice so that I could be forgiven and restored to my Father's side. Now, I could look ahead to my future with hope and confidence. My journey Home had begun!

About a week after my interview, during the pre-dawn hours, in that twilight between sleep and wakefulness, I felt a stirring in my mind that formed into a consciousness that awoke with me. The Spirit had a message from my Father. It was an invitation.

"If you want to, you can be baptized today."

Silently, I lay in bed and looked at the dark ceiling, feeling the gravitas in the thickened air around me. I turned my head to look at the time; the clock read 6:35 a.m. I wasn't sure if the prompting I had just received was true because no arrangements had been made, and I wondered if I could be baptized seemingly at the drop of a hat.

Is it possible? I decided to go for it! Now, I was too excited to go back to sleep. Getting dressed, I went downstairs to pace and putz around in the kitchen until it was a decent enough hour to call President Kenning. A little after 9:00 a.m., he answered his phone.

"Can I be baptized today?"

"Yes, if that is what you want."

I was amazed at his answer but so grateful! It humbled me to my core that my Father knew how badly I wanted to come Home to Him. I thought of Psalm 139. "If I take the wings of the morning and dwell in the uttermost parts of the sea, even there, your hand shall lead me, and your right hand shall hold me."

I felt a little guilty for putting President Kenning and so many other people to so much trouble at the last minute, but despite that, I couldn't contain my joy! I was euphoric at the thought of making my covenants with God in a few hours. President Kenning moved mountains, and I was baptized that day, in front of my children and Alan.

Father, I can rest now. I can start over with a blank slate. My sins no longer weigh me down and hold me hostage.

Afterward, my soul was finally stilled, enveloped in peace and quiet, as if I had already walked the sacred halls of the temple of my Lord and Savior. I happily settled into my new life– walking the covenant path, with my family walking it with me.

Over a year went by, and then, one day, the phone rang. It was President Kenning. It was the phone call I had been waiting for.

"Jade, I have good news for you. The Prophet told me to give you your endowments back."

Even though I had been anxiously awaiting this moment, I gasped and froze. Stammering, I said, "T-Thank you so much! How soon?"

"When do you want them back, Jade?"

I thought, *how about thirty years ago?*

As soon as we could schedule it, I was sitting in a chair in front of the desk where President Kenning was interviewing me again.

"So, Jade, before I return your endowments back to you, I'd like to ask you a question." He paused, his face somber. "Do you feel worthy?"

Suddenly, I choked up, my emotions overwhelming me, and I struggled to find the words.

"President Kenning, if I believe in the atoning blood of my Savior, and I do, then I guess I have to believe that I'm worthy."

He smiled a quiet, inward smile as if he was listening to someone else talking to him. Then, he came out from behind the desk, placed his hands upon my head, and, with the power of the priesthood, bestowed my endowments back to me. I felt a deep sense of love and belonging that I had not felt since the miracle I had experienced all those years prior, reminding me of the words that had been spoken to me in my head.

"No matter what happens to you in this life, you're going to be okay."

Grateful, I silently rejoiced. *Thank you, my Beloved Father. This life has been really hard for me. Thank you for bringing me Home.*

One of the things that changed when my blessings were restored was that the baptismal date on my membership roll was changed from my re-baptism date of December 2020, back to my original baptism date in

1985. It was as if the thirty-plus years of my wanderings on strange roads had been erased and wiped clean–just as Jesus promised.

Was it worth it to confess all my sins? Was it worth it to face the wrongs I had committed, to suffer the knowledge and recollection of them, and to know just how filthy I was before my God and Savior? The answer is absolutely *yes!* I was washed clean and restored to my covenant relationship with my Heavenly Father. And as it has been done on earth, so has it been done in heaven. I testify to you that no blessing or treasure on this earth or in heaven means more to me than this. Aside from my husband and all my children, nothing else even comes close!

A couple of months later, I made my first trip back to the temple. It had been over thirty years since I had last been there. Attending with the youth group from our church to perform baptisms, I was tearful the whole time because I was so joyful and thankful to be at my Father's house. When I participated in the confirmations at the temple following the baptisms, I noticed that the air in the small room felt thick with *presence.* It was crowded in there with the sacred press of unseen souls. I felt the keen desires of those watching and waiting, yearning to be restored to a covenant relationship with Our Father, just as I had yearned and hungered to be brought Home. Most of them had waited a lot longer than I had. How blessed I was to have reconciled with my Father while still in my mortal shell. Thank you for your great goodness and mercy to all your children, my Beloved Father!

CHAPTER 21:

Soul Reflections... and an Invitation

"Those who dance are considered insane by those who cannot hear the music."
—George Carlin

M any years ago, I was walking down an icy street in my town on a gray winter's day. Crossing the street, I saw a young woman who was smothered in a heavy coat, knitted hat, and scarf, the same as me—bundled up and struggling against the cold winter wind. She was just an ordinary person crossing the street ahead of me, walking on the same road as I. Idly, I wondered what her story was.

My soul was momentarily, but piercingly, sad. What a tragedy that I would never know who she was as a person—what her likes and dislikes were, what her life experiences had been, and what made her unique out of all the billions of souls who had ever lived on this earth. This feeling happened to me every so often as I came across a myriad of souls along my path. Sometimes, I stopped, like I did with the old man on the island during medical school, and asked questions. Often, these conversations changed my life. Most of the time, however, people passed as strangers.

I asked myself, why *are our lives so fleeting that I have been robbed of the richness that could come to my life by knowing the unique experiences and insights contained in the stories of the lives of my brothers and sisters?* At the time, I felt a deep yearning to be one with a larger collective of souls, longing to ease my feelings of separateness from others.

I believe that, through the Spirit, each of us mortals gets occasional glimpses of heaven. I recognize now that I was experiencing a yearning born from memory, a soul memory of my premortal life, where I was part of a larger collective of intelligence. The veil had left me only to see through a glass, darkly. While I couldn't remember the sum of my premortal existence, I realized I probably did know all my brothers and sisters after having had an eternity before I came here to do so. The Spirit reveals truth to us if we reach out and listen. I believe I loved all my brothers and sisters and I was surrounded by their love for me, just as I was surrounded by my Heavenly Father's love and the love of my Savior, Jesus Christ. I believe a beautiful, glorious day will come when I will remember everything. When, we all will.

What is the worth of a soul? To Our Heavenly Father and Jesus Christ, there is nothing in the universe more valuable than a soul—not the sun, the moon, or the stars in the sky. Every single one of us, even the smallest or most sinful of us, has great worth to God because we are all His sons and daughters. He has known each of us from time immemorial and loves us with the love of a perfect parent. He has dedicated His existence to us, His children. Jesus Christ, who is One with the Father, sacrificed himself so that we could be freed from the bonds of sin and death—an incomprehensible sacrifice of love—so that we might be able to return to live with Him and Our Father throughout the Eternities.

As I meet souls, and as my book goes out into the world, my deepest wish is for you to know that *you* are the reason this earth was created, that *you* are the reason our Beloved Father came up with His Plan of Salvation, and that *you* are the reason our Savior suffered and died in your place on the cross. When my children were young, there was an animated children's show on television about a magical school bus. One of the main messages on the show was to teach the children to get messy and not be afraid to make mistakes because that's how everybody learns. I would like to propose to you the idea that Earth is like a giant schoolhouse for souls. It was created as a place for Heavenly Father's children to learn, make mistakes, and grow. And that it's okay to be human and get messy because that is how we learn.

Making mistakes and facing the consequences of those mistakes is how we grow and make progress in our journey to become like our Heavenly Father. We partake of the tree of the knowledge of good and evil. And we learn to distinguish between good and evil, darkness and light, through our mortal experiences. We can learn how to choose the good.

As we make messes and learn, who cleans up the messes we make? I believe His name is Jesus Christ. Why do we need Him? Because there are some messes we cannot clean up. We simply cannot. We don't know how to fix them, and we don't have the ability to fix them. But He has promised to fix them for us.

There are some wounds that only He can heal. And we have been bought and redeemed with a terrible price that only He could pay for us. He will put everything right one day. All our hurts and pains will be healed. Justice and mercy will be done. And as we go off to His Kingdom of Glory, I believe there will be peace. There will be love and happiness for all of Father's children.

Our present life on this earth is not our destiny. Our destiny is so much grander than we can possibly imagine right now. For, after all, we are of royal descent. Our destiny is to become as He is; we are his sons and daughters. Because of His infinite love and tender mercy toward us, our happiness is assured.

While Jesus Christ is inviting us to be inheritors with Him in Our Father's kingdom, I believe that one of the main problems standing in our way is that we are living in a world that demands that we hurry up, go faster and faster, with little time to clearly see the road on which we are traveling. This is what I did. I stayed so busy that I could not face my own demons, and it spurred me to rebel against people in my life, which led me to rebel against my God. Blinded by my anger and bitterness, I practically raced down that path! Have you done this, too? When we get too busy, it begs a question:

Do we even know if it is a road we want to travel on?

Too many distractions in life can numb us to the point that we don't realize where we are going or the consequences of following the path we've chosen.

I have learned that time is running out for all of us. The clock's ticking. None of us know when the last day of our mortal life will arrive. We don't know the day of the Second Coming of Our Lord Jesus Christ or the day of our last breath on earth. Both days are the end of the game for us—the end of our mortal probation. When that day comes, the final exam will be over, and we will receive the grade for the school year. I've come to realize that each of us chooses how we will spend the rest of eternity.

I have also learned not to allow someone else's boorish, obnoxious, or toxic behavior, both inside and outside of the church, to affect my relationship with my Heavenly Father. There's no point in becoming offended or hurt by someone else's unfair behavior to the point that a person stops coming to church. Why should I and my future generations be robbed of the blessings my Father has in store for us?

The reality is that people are imperfect beings. There are some tares amongst the wheat in all churches. I have learned to deal with it, reminding myself that we cannot control other people's behaviors, but we have the freedom to choose our own.

Realize your true potential! *You are greater than you can imagine right now, greater than you can remember.* Don't ever settle to be less than who you can be—a true child of God. I have now started over. Having lived as I have, I now know we can each start over, every day. Under all the superficial barriers and masks we wear, we are more alike than we are different. And nothing speaks louder or with more ripples in a pond than a shared personal experience.

As I wrote this book, I accepted that it was not a comfortable feeling for me to expose my weaknesses, imperfections, and mistakes. Obviously, I've made some humdingers! But I've felt that it was important to share my mistakes with you because, as people, we often learn from each other and understand ourselves better through each other's stories. We can feel a sense of unity, knowing that someone else has had at least an idea of our struggles, so we don't feel alone anymore. If nothing else, maybe the story of my life can serve as a warning to others. Although salvation is an individual experience, exaltation is truly a collective experience. We need each other.

As I have moved forward on my path, trusting in His will and His timing for me, I have learned to turn *toward* God rather than *away* from Him amid my trials and disappointments. While I still struggle, I offer Him my struggle. Our struggles to be more in line with God are the offerings we give to our Savior as we pick up our crosses of frailties, inclinations, trials, and adversities. I am encouraged by the thought that as I struggle, I am slowly becoming sculpted by the potter, becoming a new creature in Christ, and by doing so, I am no longer held in bondage to my younger self. My past no longer chains me, and I am free to walk a different road than the roads I once wandered.

Although this might be controversial, I believe that many, if not all the issues we encounter in this life were "custom-made" for us to experience in mortality. Not that God does bad things to us, but He knows the past, present, and future. He has known each of us as individual souls for an eternity before we were born into a mortal world. He knows exactly what experiences we need *to grow us*—to become more like Him. You may disagree with me, and that's okay, but I have come to believe that we are placed by time, birth, and geography into a life where we encounter different situations, tests, and experiences that will give us the maximum opportunities to learn and grow.

We are all unique individuals, and need different experiences to grow. That's why our tests and trials in this life are different for each of us. God has created a purpose and a plan for each soul. I have learned firsthand that no one is unimportant or invisible to Him. Even if we think we are insignificant, we may unknowingly be playing a critical role in Father's Great

Plan! I believe our Father will accomplish His perfect work through His imperfect children.

The crucial questions are: *Are we all in? What has our salvation cost us? What are we willing to put on the altar before God?*

As I pray on my knees, humbly placing all that I am on the altar before Him, I consecrate all my sins and suffering, as well as my talents and time, my labor and longings, to Him. May He use my life in whatever way He sees fit to bring forth His designs and purposes.

Sometimes, I picture myself as a little cotter pin, holding a tiny wheel onto a larger wheel that is attached to a larger wheel that is attached to an even larger one, *ad infinitum*. Wheels within wheels. I am but a tiny, infinitesimal part of the vast machinery of the universe that my Heavenly Father has created. May God take my small and imperfect efforts and magnify them. I testify that Jesus Christ, our Savior and Redeemer, is the Good Shepherd who leaves the righteous sheep to search out the wayward ones who, like me, have wandered away... to bring them Home. And this I know—there is room for you at His table of blessings.

I want God's blessings for my children, grandchildren, great-grandchildren, and future generations. As I have learned from my prodigal daughter experience, there is no real or lasting joy to be found outside of a covenant with God—only broken dreams, broken lives, and broken people. I have realized that it doesn't matter how much money you have, how educated you are, or how much you have risen to the top in your career. When we each stand before the judgment seat of the Great Jehovah, the only thing that will matter is if we have shown the love to others that our Heavenly Father and Jesus Christ have shown to us.

I have many regrets about my life and the decisions I have made, but I have also learned a lot from my mistakes. When I was acting out in anger and rebellion, I not only hurt other people, but I also hurt myself. It has taken years of following a more moral lifestyle to recoup any measure of peace in my heart. I could have made other choices to deal with my earlier suffering than the ones I made. Instead, I reaped the consequences.

I also regret that I wasn't a better friend to those I encountered in my life. My experiences with childhood bullying and the other circumstances of my childhood left me with a deep sense of distrust, separateness, and loneliness that I carried through my whole life until I met my husband, Alan. Then, the burden of my exile to the wilderness began to lift from me. Until Alan, I have rarely trusted anyone to take care of me or not hurt me.

Even though Alan hasn't been baptized to become a member of my church, he has learned, listened, and chooses, on his own, to follow the commandments. Depending on his busy work schedule, he attends church services with our children and me as often as he can and participates in church activities. When they expressed a desire, he supported our four children being baptized and attended all their baptisms. Alan pays a generous fast offering and tithing monthly, drives me to the temple on his way to do medical rounds on his patients, and picks me up when I am done. He also stopped drinking alcohol and coffee of his own accord. By these and many more of his actions, he shows me that he loves his children and me every single day. Still no saint (like the rest of us), I couldn't ask for a sweeter or gentler husband. Hopefully, he will choose to be baptized one day, and we can be sealed together in the temple. I want to spend eternity with him and our family.

One of my biggest lessons over time was to realize that my Heavenly Father and Jesus Christ have always been there, moving behind the scenes of my life. They have been watching me carefully from the background, involved in my pain and sorrows, encouraging me to do better, but letting me make my own decisions. Father never stopped trying to let me know how much He loves me, especially when I didn't feel lovable or choose what He perhaps would have wanted me to do.

The first extraordinary miracle I experienced that saved my life didn't change the circumstances I was suffering. The suffering continued until the time that it was measured for ended. Even though I prayed for God to change some of the people in my life, I've learned that God *doesn't* make people change. It must be their choice. But the memory of that miracle, the comfort of knowing that I was going to be okay, no matter what happened to me in my life, and the love I felt from my Heavenly Father continues to hold me up. I experience less times of panic and despair.

So, are we all in? In the Holy Scriptures, there is the story of a widow who gave only two small coins as an offering, compared to many wealthier people who gave so much more money. Jesus stated that He found her contribution more acceptable to Him than all the other people's contributions because those people gave out of their surplus; she gave all she had (Mark 12: 41-44). My beloved, He is asking you to give all you have. He is asking you to lay on the altar before Him, our Beloved Lord and Savior, all that is good about you, as well as your faults and imperfections, so that He may wash you clean. Our individual struggles to follow Him are our sacrifices to Him. He asks us to come to Him as we are.

As the Creator of All, everything belongs to Him, except the agency that He gifted each of us—our ability to choose. So, what do you give to the One who has everything? This question brings the problem of Christmas shopping up to a whole new level! The only true gift that is ours to give to our Heavenly Father is our heart. Our choice to give Him the gift of a contrite spirit and a broken heart is more precious to Him than all the gold and riches in the universe. It is a simple act of love, freely given to One who has given so much more to us.

My dearly beloved friend, can we hear the music? Will we be one of those who can sing the song of redeeming love on The Great Day of His Coming? (Alma 5:26) Come, let us follow Him, for the road that He guides us to leads us Home.

EPILOGUE:

Puzzles

"My dear brothers and sisters,
the length of your life is not as important as the kind of life that you live.
For each of us, even for a 100-year-old man, life passes quickly. My
prayer is that you will let God prevail in your life. Make covenants with
Him. Stay on the covenant path. Prepare to return to live with Him again."
—Russell M. Nelson

Recently, during one pre-holiday season, I placed folding tables in our living room and set out puzzles and games for my children to play with. They were on school break, and my husband and I would join them, having fun and laughing, in the evenings when we were all together. I would lovingly giggle, watching the changing emotions on their rapt young faces as they groaned ruefully when they lost a game or struggled mightily to find the right puzzle piece, their concentration intense. My heart felt as if it would burst with joy and gratitude. They just don't know how beautiful and wonderfully made they are!

All too soon, it would be time to clean up and prepare for bed because we had more grand adventures planned the next day.

It's hard for me to believe that after the life I have lived, this is where I have arrived on my long journey so far. Life can often be unexpected. *I didn't see this beautiful life coming!* It's too bad we can't see around corners.

Upon writing this book, I was puzzled by what to include and what to exclude in the story of a life. Looking through the puzzle pieces, I see places where the cardboard is bent, creased, and worn. Some pieces don't fit quite as well as they used to in the spot they were designed for. Time takes a toll on us all. Some of the shiny surface of the puzzle picture has peeled or rubbed off, making what used to be there murky and muddled. In other spots, there are gaps where pieces are missing. What used to be there is gone, and I feel those empty spaces in my life.

Even though I have found happiness since returning to the Church of Jesus Christ of Latter-day Saints, and although the heavens have opened and my Father has poured out His blessings upon me, my life is not perfect. Still, I feel that my life is as close to a heaven on earth as is possible in this world of opposites.

As I have been sharing and talking to others who have wandered down strange roads, I couldn't promise them a magic potion that would suddenly change everything. Yet, I continue believing in the power of Jesus Christ's atoning sacrifice to work miracles in our lives. Miracles do happen every day.

These ordinary, everyday miracles often happen quietly over time. They can happen so subtly that we might not notice the change until we come out the other side and realize we are free. Free from hurt, free from anger, free from self-loathing, and free from shame. For we can have our robes washed white in the redeeming blood of the Lamb.

I have seen His quiet, unobtrusive miracles at work in my life, daily, and that of my children. His tender mercies carefully unfold, slowly blooming like a lotus emerging from the mud to unfold into a beautiful flower. His forgiveness is the grace of clear water—the meandering stream which embraces the rocks it curls itself around on its journey, rippling and sparkling in the sun, carefully and gently bringing us Home.

One of the main takeaways I have learned, as I look back at the puzzle of my life, is that President Kenning was right.

It matters how you treat people. It really matters.

I believe if we can learn only one lesson in this life, it will be enough if we understand that *it matters how we treat people, including ourselves.* When we learn that, we will finally become enough.

No matter who we are or where we come from, it's important to know that we have a Home with God. It doesn't matter which faith path we follow, as long as we follow Him. There are more than eight billion people in the world today. That means God has more than eight billion ways to reach us. What matters is our reaching back.

In regards to the community of Christ's family that doesn't look exactly like the heterosexual community, I can tell you that this is a worldwide phenomenon that everyone must face, as it is happening amongst nearly every family in every background. I can only share with you the importance of coming forward with as much Christlike love and compassion as we can each muster as individuals. Remember, it matters how you treat people.

In summation, I have come to realize that it's not about our mistakes; it's about our repentance and the good things we choose to do now. It's about our *struggles* to stay on the covenant path and our constant striving, learning, and growing. He wants us to change and become more like Him.

And if we let Him, He will burn off our imperfections to reveal the true gold underneath.

There are battles that rage every day on this earth for the souls of humanity. There are many reasons why too many of us have left our churches. The fear of missing out on all the shiny, glittery things that beckon can lure someone from the covenant path. As for me, I am done with being a fish on a hook. Instead of feeling FOMO (the Fear Of Missing Out), I've learned that it might be better to focus on JOMO (the Joy Of Missing Out) *because not all that glitters is gold!* Walking the covenant path again has helped me to feel the joy of missing out—on all the chaos, trouble, sorrow, and heartache of living in the Wilderness!

If you're like me, you might say that life has been extremely hard. That's how it is in this mortal world. But there will come a day, soon, when Father will come into the room and tell us to put the game away. Fold the game board up, stack the deck of cards, gather up the tokens, put everything back in the box, and put it away. Because we are going to other places, and we will have other things to do. The adventure will continue somewhere else. Please, come with us.

"My actions speak louder than mere words.
My life is my testimony."
—Jade Oster

Acknowledgments

To my wonderful husband, Alan, and my children. You are the reason for my hope in a better future, a new world, and life everlasting.

To Sister Sherrie Waite, an inspiring leader in our church and the host of our women's monthly Book Club. I'll never forget how, after I gave a talk in church one day, you asked me, "Jade, have you ever considered becoming an author?" My eyes opened wide, and I huffed, surprised, "Oh, that's not going to happen!" Sherrie, I would like to say I was wrong, and you were right.

To Sister Melissa Franson, who came over to my house with her children and the missionaries to clean my overgrown yard. You have no idea what an impact you had on me. Other than the missionaries, you were my first introduction to a member of the church when I came home. Later, you offered me my first calling, teaching Primary. You are proof that even a small act of kindness can move universes throughout the Eternities.

To my dear Sister Kim Pace, I have enjoyed your company so much! You are my fellow co-conspirator and co-fashionista as we have oohed and aahed over our latest shopping finds. Thank you so much for bringing fun and laughter into my life as we giggled like schoolgirls over shoe designs. Thank you for being my friend.

To my dearest friends in Corbin, Kentucky ward, Lexington Stake, and around the world. I love you. Thank you for doing all that you do to help Father gather His children Home. When I was young and hurt, my credo was, "He who travels fastest travels alone." Now that I am older and know I am loved, I have realized, "He who travels the farthest travels with others."

I can't go Home without you. The road is too long and difficult for me to travel by myself. I need you all. Thank you for coming with me.

To all the leaders in Zion, from our beloved Prophet, Russell M. Nelson, and our apostles, to our missionaries of all ages the world over, as well as those called to serve in our stakes and wards. You, who have dedicated your lives to us in service, my heart is forever yours. At times, your flock can be an unruly bunch of sheep who seem to be constantly in danger from all manner of misadventures. Thank you for your vigilance and sleepless nights of prayer.

I thank you, my beloved Father, for the precious gift of your only-begotten Son. I know that you and your son are One in thought and deed. I thank you, my eldest brother, Jesus, for your infinite, atoning sacrifice on behalf of all your younger brothers and sisters. I know you constantly stand before our Father's throne, advocating for us with the Father, with mercy and justice. I love you, and I will follow you forever. I want to make you proud of me. I don't want the blood you shed for me to have no purchase in my heart. Although the veil parts us, and I have no memory of your dear, sweet face, my heart tells me that long ago, when I was a small spirit child, I walked with you on starlit, cosmic paths, basking in your love. Smiling, I held your hand and said to you, "Teach me, O Lord, and raise me up to be a servant unto thee, for I will serve my God."

"And there were many who were lost from his view,
wandering in strange roads."
—from Lehi's vision

A Very Special Thanks

"To write is human. To edit is divine."
—Stephen King

I would very much like to thank Rebecca Hall Gruyter of Your Purpose Driven Practice and Bridget Cook-Burch of Your Inspired Story and their amazing teams for editing and publishing my book. I was absolutely clueless when I turned in my "finished" manuscript to them, vastly unaware that books are not written; they are rewritten. (And rewritten, and rewritten, and rewritten...)

In writing my book, I learned just how badly my grammar sucks. I thank God for my lovely editors who were tirelessly patient with me, coaching and encouraging me to put forth my best efforts. My book would not be anywhere close to what I wanted it to be without their endless attention to detail.

A fond and heartfelt thanks to my Beta Readers: Karen Munson, Wendy Bowers, Janet Cheney, and Alan Oster. My book is so much better because of your vital and honest feedback.

Although I am not sponsored by any of the following wonderful people, I would like to give credit where credit is due. Photographs of Jade are by Keshia Amburgey of Keshia Amburgey Photography, London, Kentucky. Jade's color, cut, and style are by Donna Thomas of Looks to Kill Salon, Corbin, Kentucky. Jade's manicure is by Rose Tran and Mike Nguyen of Super Nails, London, Kentucky. Jade's eyebrows are by Kimberly Tran of

The Babe Cave, Lexington and London, Kentucky. Jade's lips are by Cody Michael of Ivy and Grace, Lexington, Kentucky. A warm thanks to David Harris and his elite team of trainers at Protection Dog Sales, Frankfort, Kentucky, for my four protection "fuzzy bears." My family would not be complete without them! Photograph of Kenna and Yelena is by Jessica and Lance Dickert of Protection Dog Sales and Rockcastle Canine Training Center, Mount Vernon, Kentucky.

Jade Oster

About the Author

J ade is an author, speaker, and advocate for the underdog. Throughout her life, she worked at homeless teen shelters, gave HIV-AIDS educational instruction at high schools, co-ran an HIV hotline at her university at the height of the AIDS epidemic, volunteered at a free women's clinic in downtown Minneapolis for the underprivileged, and volunteered at an AIDS hospice.

Once a former E-4 specialist in active-duty Army and Reserves, she switched directions and earned her ASN from Gordon College of Nursing in Georgia and her BSN at Metropolitan State University in Minnesota. She went on to earn her Doctorate of Medicine from Ross University School of Medicine in the Commonwealth of Dominica.

Jade traveled "strange roads" but found bliss later in life with her husband, Alan. After the miracle of being able to be a mother again at age fifty, she loved staying home with her four young children. With her overabundance of energy, she earned her real estate license and learned how to develop property. She is the proud mother of eight children in a blended family, and she is very active in her church and her testimony of Christ.

Jade has a rescue cat named *Potato Gouda,* who came to her with a wire sticking out of his jaw. After spending $700 on vet bills, the cat became hers. Now semi-retired, Jade loves to read, write, educate herself from the University of YouTube, train her two rescue dogs, *Rocky Balboa* and *Twinkie,* and especially her four German Shepherd protection pups, *Kenna,*

Dylan, Sniper, and *Yelena.* They are "fuzzy bears" but prepared to protect. Of course, the rescue, Twinkie, is the one with attitude. She thinks she is married to Jade's beloved husband, Alan, and sees Jade as "the help."

Message from the Author

Fellow travelers, sometimes we need a friend to talk to on our way
Home. Let me know if I can ever be of support to you.
Contact me at http://www.JadeOsterJadeInk.com
as well as at my email: JadeOsterJadeInk@gmail.com

Reviews

"What a beautiful life lived! Jade's story is a testament to tenacity, resilience, and self-belief. Her journey inspires anyone who feels lost or overwhelmed by life's challenges. The deep generational bond between Jade, her mother, and her daughters is a beautiful reminder that love's enduring presence is potent and powerful in catalyzing personal growth and self-realization. This book celebrates individual strength, family connections, and the enduring power of love, leaving readers with a renewed sense of hope and courage."
—Wendy Beth, Soul Guide, and Author

"Jade is immensely brave and courageous to be willing to tell her story. I love her heart. It is evident from the beginning that Jade was a very hurt little girl who always wanted what was right and good. Thank you Jade for sharing, for being vulnerable, for your strong testimony."
—Karen Munson, Author

"This autobiography is a powerful journey through the trials and triumphs of her life, capturing the essence of resilience and hope. From a challenging childhood to overcoming hardships as an adult, her story is a testament to the human spirit. Her candid writing invites readers to share her struggles and celebrate her growth, leaving an indelible mark of inspiration. This book is more than just a recounting of her life. It's a beacon of strength for anyone facing their own battles. Her story has inspired me and given me strength and hope to persevere through my own struggles. Thank you, Jade!"
—Patti Ogden, Mother, Psychology and Social Work Double Major

"Overall, I thought Jade's story was interesting and heartfelt. She had courage in drudging up painful memories and the perseverance to make her life and the life of her children better.
The message I took away from reading Jade's story was that regardless of how many sewer traps you fall in, God will pull you out if you reach out."
—Anonymous

"This is a book of hurts, disappointments, mistakes, and a deep inner knowing of traveling the wrong road that prevented the author, Jade, from hearing the music. She invites us into her painful journey that stole her peace for years. She shares how impossible it was to clearly see the road she was travelling—she was too busy pushing herself to fill every moment of everyday to avoid hurtful memories, while trying to survive.
But it is also a book of courage, strength, and how she "yearned and hungered" to find her way back to God and hear the music. As Jade found forgiveness from God and from herself, she reminds us that our experiences shape our lives. Her journey helps us to know that as we learn and grow from our own experiences, we can create opportunities to start a new and fresh life. Starting over, in her own words, she had to "remember to forget," a strong message for the reader struggling with hurtful memories that have become a constant companion. Jade's story of starting her new journey, accepting forgiveness, and remembering to forget lets the reader know that surely, we can do it also."
—Claudean Oakley, Author, Speaker and Trainer